DO NOT REMOVE
CARDS FROM POCKET

9/30/93

ALLEN COUNTY PUBLIC LIBRARY
FORT WAYNE, INDIANA 46802

You may return this book to any agency, branch,
or bookmobile of the Allen County Public Library.

DEMCO

An Hour
Before Dawn

An Hour Before Dawn

Dennis Anderson

Voyageur Press

Edited by Jane McHughen
Cover designed by Zachary J. Marell
Book designed by Helene Anderson

Printed in the United States of America
93 94 95 96 97 5 4 3 2 1

Library of Congress Cataloging-in-Publication Data
  Anderson, Dennis, 1951–
    An hour before dawn : stories of the outdoors / Dennis Anderson.
        p. cm.
    ISBN 0-89658-180-2
    1. Natural history—Outdoor books. 2. Hunting. 3. Duck shooting.
  I. Title
  QH81.A565   1993   92-41227
  508—dc20   CIP

Published by
Voyageur Press, Inc.
P.O. Box 338, 123 North Second Street
Stillwater, MN 55082 U.S.A.
From Minnesota and Canada 612-430-2210
Toll-free 800-888-9653

Voyageur Press books are also available at discounts for quantities for educational, fundraising, premium, or sales-promotion use. For details contact the marketing department. Please write or call for our free catalog of natural history publications.

Acknowledgments

This book is the culmination of many efforts and interests, and I am particularly grateful to my editors at the *Pioneer Press*; to my friends who regularly allow me amplification rights to their lives; to readers whose advice oftentimes is valuable; to my families, extended and immediate; and particularly to my wife, Jan, and the various dogs, horses, and barn cats we support, all of whom make our lives interesting.

Contents

Empty Skies: America's Ducks in Crisis

Introduction

An *Hour Before Dawn* is a collection of stories and columns about the outdoors that appeared in the St. Paul *Pioneer Press* during an approximately 10-year period, beginning in 1980. Some are tales whose geographical focus is Minnesota, Wisconsin, or other states of the Upper Midwest; others carry datelines from the Caribbean, Alaska, and Louisiana.

My travels were made at the expense of my editors, whose budgets and good humor have supported my journeys, the newsroom justification of which must, in the end, be stories in which readers have an interest. Some of these concern fishing, others hunting, still others dogs and horses. The hope is that the subjects chosen are ones the curious and venturesome will find inviting.

Stories appearing in the first part of this book are not grounded in specific time periods and have been reworked slightly from their original form so that one follows the next in the fashion of book chapters. Ambitiously perhaps, my initial intent in writing them was not to portray detail-by-detail the mechanics of fly-casting or other outdoor skills, the hook-and-bullet aspects of outdoor writing having, I think, been given sufficient airing over the years. Rather, I hoped the more universal themes of friendship and challenge, intrigue and accomplishment could be visited successfully, and perhaps from these readers could draw parallels to their own outdoor undertakings, real or imagined.

The second part of the book comprises a series of stories I wrote in 1988 entitled "Empty Skies: America's Ducks in Crisis." The articles were the fruit of a year-long attempt to document in as comprehensive a way as possible reasons for the more than 60 percent decline in North American duck numbers since the 1940s.

The subject was important to me because I had experienced the decline first-hand, watching autumn upon autumn, even as recently as the 1970s, as duck populations fell, seemingly precipitously. Everyone had their own read on the problem, from federal waterfowl managers to Ducks Unlimited biologists to the guy down the street, who oftentimes also returned from hunts frustrated if not saddened about the loss of birds—a loss which, perhaps, portended more serious life changes to come.

The first stories in this project arose from the mud of Louisiana's bayous. It was there that I traveled to document as best I could the extent of the illegal kill of waterfowl in Louisiana. Of all the "Empty Skies" stories written in 1988, these, it seems, have been the most widely remembered, primarily for the portrayals of vast numbers of ducks killed illegally by some Louisiana hunters. It is important to remember, however, that, as my friend Ace Cullum of Monroe, Louisiana, himself a one-time violator, is fond of saying, "Louisiana has all the duck killers because Louisiana has all the ducks." Meaning Louisiana has been unique traditionally only in the scope of its illegal waterfowl kill. Pare away the big numbers, and other wingshots in most other states stand no less guilty.

Overbagging stories were also written in 1988 from Mexico, Texas, and elsewhere, but so, too, were stories of habitat loss and waterfowl population mismanagement, and of drought. Add to these modern agriculture's reliance on pesticides and herbicides, and credit must be given any duck still aloft in the 1990s.

Stories from "Empty Skies" published here are in their original form. Readers should know that since the articles' first appearance, considerable progress has been made on a number of fronts. Louisiana, thanks in

11

no small part to the efforts of U.S. Fish and Wildlife Service special agent Dave Hall and other state and federal agents, as well as former Governor Buddy Roemer and former Louisiana Wildlife and Fisheries Secretary Virginia Van Sickle, has become a leader among states in waterfowl law enforcement. Also, sincere efforts are being made in Mexico, spearheaded by Ducks Unlimited, to curb overbagging there by visiting American gunners. Moreover, Ducks Unlimited has in effect transformed itself from a group that rarely preached the gospel of ethical hunting to one that now confronts the subject regularly.

Whether these and other efforts will contribute to a rebounding of North American duck numbers is anyone's guess. America's callous attitude toward wetlands, its dependence on clean farming, and its eroding agrarian base argue that times will continue to be tough for ducks in years to come.

Dennis Anderson
January 1993
St. Paul

Going Home

I was born on North Dakota's prairies but grew up in northern Michigan's woods, a conflicting influence of geography that places me, in the idealistic imaginings of my retirement, in Minnesota, on a farm somewhere near Ortonville and on a lake just outside of Ely.

Psychologically, the expansiveness of the former setting features a type of wide-open inspiration the latter lacks. You know, possibilities. But clusters of pine and birch offer security, which is why if my ship ever comes in I'll take options on property in both locales; lay up reasonable quantities of venison, fish, and fowl at each site; and pass my last days slowly, commuting from place to place, north to south and back again.

The issue arose with particular urgency when I made a trip to Gladstone, in the Upper Peninsula of Michigan, for a high school reunion, my 20th. Not having family there anymore (and haven't for as long as I've been out of high school), the pilgrimage was, for me, a rare one. So much so that I undertook it with the unease of an interloper, one whose sense of belonging to the community was tethered tenuously, as though by a fly fisherman's tippet—that final stretch of monofilament that connects fly to fly line.

Nevertheless, the trip was made, and by vehicle, too, flying having been ruled out because it lacks the opportunity for slow decompression that only ground travel permits. As Thomas Wolfe has pointed out, the past is best reentered warily, as if stepping into a bath of unknown temperature.

So, on the designated day, I loaded two dogs into the back of the truck, gave them a brief outline of the venture at hand (their sighs, I thought, were audible), and pointed the whole outfit to the east, moving not slowly, perhaps, but deliberately.

When I was young, the world stretched before me like two-lane blacktop, and I, together with a handful of my friends, came out of high school's dark chute eager to lay down some rubber. The game plan, as we saw it, was one of get up and go, of placing chips accumulated during our formative years on all available numbers, with fairly hot motorcycles and not-quite-cool-enough cars providing the transportation.

For the moment, the fishing and hunting that are a part of most anyone's life in the Upper Peninsula were put on hold. Well past were the days when as kids we would spend long mornings and even longer afternoons fishing from the dilapidated town pier or, not far away, in the "lagoon," this last being a murky stretch of water that snakes out of the Gladstone harbor, offering untold recreational opportunities to small-town kids bent on catching a few perch or, better yet, wading into and through what a fisheries biologist might call "emergent vegetation"—and vast quantities of it at that.

The harbor itself offered a different form of entertainment. It was a safe haven for Lake Michigan navigators, and as a kid I would watch in wonder at the comings and goings of all manner of boats, hometown as well as transient. Across the shiny mahogany sterns of some were names like *Misty* and *Enchanted*. Also inscribed were "Benton Harbor" and "Chicago" and "Green Bay," home ports for the wayfaring public who somehow discovered Gladstone on their maps and decided this would be the summer to visit.

My father liked to fish, and when he got a little ahead of the game moneywise he invested in a 14-foot Crestliner boat, which he teamed with a 1958 7½-horsepower Johnson. In winter he stored the motor in the basement. Outside, in the backyard, he turned the boat over, straddling it across two sawhorses. Sometimes in March and early April I would see him staring out the kitchen window at the Crestliner, still piled high with snow, counting the days, I'm sure, until he could again launch the boat in one of the many inland lakes nearby and, on calm mornings, in the more protected waters of Lake Michigan's Little Bay de Noc.

Our family camped some too, and on weekends the boat would be hoisted atop a pop-up tent trailer, tied down, and the whole unit linked to a '57 Chev station wagon. A favorite destination was Garden Lake, 60 or so miles away, the distance of which Dad covered with his left hand holding the steering wheel while with his right he flailed about in the general direction of the back seat, trying to prevent my older brother from punching me senseless. "He's doing it again, Dad!" I would yell, words that would bring my father's right arm over the seat back, while my brother attempted to scrunch out of reach, all the while pleading his innocence and waiting for yet another opportunity to practice a little brotherly assault and battery.

Come fall, my father, brother, and I would hunt deer; sometimes ruffed grouse, too. But mostly Dad was a duck hunter. And duck hunters, being a breed unto themselves, often find little patience for hunting forest birds, the cloistered environment of a hunt in the woods just not being the same as that of a hunt undertaken in, say, the vast wheat stubble that surrounds Rugby, North Dakota. We moved from Rugby to Gladstone in my fifth year of grade school.

My earliest memories are of duck hunting in North Dakota. My father had a big black Lab named Boze, and in summer, in preparation for the coming waterfowl migration, Dad would put Boze in the trunk of the company car and out into the North Dakota countryside we would go, the point being to get Boze into shape.

No fool, Boze was hip to the agenda. When the car stopped he knew the trunk would be coming open and he would be free once again to run road ditches with abandon. For maybe five miles, he would trail the car, grinning, while I, head turned back, watched from the passenger seat, and Dad, smoking a filterless Camel, eyed the rearview mirror.

When the waterfowl season finally began and the North Dakota skies filled with mallards and wigeon and shovelers and geese—hundreds of thousands of snows and blues and Canadas—my father would break out his Remington semiauto and, for him, life would begin anew. On many of his hunting trips, my brother and I were allowed to come along, sometimes to handle Boze, sometimes to help dig pits, sometimes to find mallards downed in picked cornfields. But I suspect mostly we were invited because my father figured the experience would have a beneficial effect on his two boys, or at least that's the thought that occurred to me not many years ago while duck hunting on Lake of the Woods with, among other friends, my brother.

Then one day Dad said we were moving to Michigan. We were moving to Michigan, he said, and that was that.

Some time later, my mother got out an encyclopedia, and she and I and my brother stared at a map of what would become our new home. Later Dad joined in and, in a voice that trailed off noticeably, mentioned that while Michigan had some ducks it could not compare in that respect to North Dakota and that therefore he was selling his Remington semiauto.

What's more, he said, Boze would be going to a friend of his up near the Canadian border, a man who could hunt the big Lab in the fall as much as a dog of his experience and caliber needed to be hunted.

"You don't take a dog like Boze and move him to Michigan, where there are no ducks," Dad said. "It wouldn't be right."

And so a clean break was made.

Now, seven or so hours after leaving home, I am within a few hundred yards of the Gladstone Yacht Club. Inside are many, if not most, of the kids I grew up with, some of whom I have not seen for two decades.

Wanting to exercise the dogs a final time, I drop the tailgate, free them of their cages, and point them in the direction of a nearby ball diamond. Beyond is the big lake, and I repeatedly admonish the dogs not to roll in any dead fish that may have washed ashore. Then I say, "Live it up," and watch as the two Labs, both black, scamper across the infield and into the dark water.

In the diffused light of the distant yacht club parking lot I see all manner of cars, but no motorcycles: no Harley Davidsons, not even a Honda.

As kids my friend Craig Johnson and I rode 305 Scramblers—his a Yamaha, mine a Honda—into and out of untold weird situations. Later, we ratcheted our investments up a few notches, he purchasing a 750 Honda and I a Harley Sportster. One summer we rode to San Francisco, making it all the way to Elko, Nevada, before running out of money. Had we not sold rides to kids at the local Dairy Queen for 50 cents a pop, we might not have made it to the coast.

Still looking at the parking lot, I see no Corvairs, the machine of choice for one David Kee, circa 1968; no Rambler Classics, the vehicle with the fold-down seats; or hopped-up Mustangs, which Bob Gustafson knew something about. Instead, there is only the usual accumulation of wheels, sedans mostly—some foreign, some domestic—and way too few pickups.

Whistling the dogs to heel, I put them up for the night. Then I move the truck the short distance to the parking lot and step out into the cool evening. A dank breeze is aloft off the lake. The harbor is nearly full with pretty big boats. Two kids row a beat-up dinghy in disjointed syncopation. And "Good Thing," a song by the Fine Young Cannibals, drifts through the air like smoke, perhaps from a stereo in one of the bigger boats. I think: OK.

17

Over the next 24 hours I will learn that no one in our class of some 125 kids has died, that Craig Johnson is now a lawyer in Portland, Oregon, who hunts and fishes; that Ed Hart, in addition to working "down-state" for Oldsmobile, owns a bird dog kennel; that David Kee lives in the country, across the bay, on the Stonington Peninsula; that John Louis knows where there's some pretty good woodcock shooting near Houghton, Michigan; and that Bruce Richards, who lives in Florida, couldn't make it to the reunion because he has only two weeks of vacation and "needs them for deer hunting."

But that good news and good news about the rest of my classmates will come later. For now, I'm content to absorb the scene that is the harbor, the lagoon, and—in the distance—the bay, where a small sailboat has just come about, tacking toward the distant lights of Escanaba, Gladstone's subordinate sister city.

It all looks good, and for the moment there is not even the slightest hint of disappointments of the past 20 years: of cancer taking Dad, of friends won and lost, of things that might have been but weren't.

I open the yacht club door, prepared to order a tall glass of tanglefoot and let the chips fall where they may.

As I do, I think: Going home ain't so bad.

Birds and Hutterites
in Alberta

An hour before dawn and Willy boy was cold. The hood of his parka was turned against an early-winter wind that cut across the Canadian prairie like a bad omen. He reached for his thermos to pour a cup of coffee, then dropped a shoulder and hunkered still lower into the snowy wheat stubble, focusing his eyes on the steam that drifted from the insulated cup. Twenty yards away, two dozen decoys stood motionless, sentries in the dark.

"It'll be a while," Willy boy said.

I knew as much. So did Sage, the Lab that lay outside the blind, ears perked in the direction of the lake in the middle distance; a lake that held so many geese and ducks and swans that when time came to lift from the water and fly to nearby fields to feed, tens of thousands of chortling birds, wings beating icy air almost vengefully, would fill the sky in every direction.

Destination: cruising altitude.

There were no other hunters, not for sections of land in every direction. "Everybody's done," a Hutterite man had said. "Too cold. Winter's coming."

Hutterites.

The question, "What gives?" comes to mind if you stumble onto one of their prairie colonies. Women in bonnets and long black skirts. Men in black coats and caps reminiscent of those worn in the Civil War.

All living together.

Section after section, Hutterites own almost all the land in this particular part of Alberta near Stettler, a fact Willy boy and I noted when we were directed to a man others in the colony said was their leader.

Willy boy: "We'd like to hunt your land if we could."

The man, who was overseeing the building of a new sheep shed, looked at Willy boy.

Then he looked at me.

The man asked: "Where you from?"

"Minnesota."

"No birds in Minnesota?"

"Thought we'd try something different."

Which was true. But what was also true was this: If you have not watched too much TV and therefore possess at least some of your senses, the chance to be on far-northern prairies to meet the coming of winter and the last migrants it pushes out of the high Arctic is one you don't pass up. Assuming correct timing—mid to late October—bitter weather and the birds it brings with it will wash over you in waves, speckled-belly geese and Canada geese and snow geese and mallards reluctantly yielding to winter the land of their birth and nurturing; evicted, finally, by freezing temperatures and slanting snow and wind so harsh it can muffle the blast of a 12-gauge.

Two more Hutterite men joined the conversation.

Then the Hutterite leader said: "Hunt any of our land you want. Just close the gates. And don't leave anything behind."

So now Willy boy and I were looking for geese. In this part of Alberta, a two-hour drive south of Edmonton, there are upland birds as well as waterfowl: Hungarian partridge, sharp-tailed grouse, ruffed grouse, even pheasants. And on previous days we had hunted these—Huns and sharps mostly—trailing behind Risky, an English setter, as she worked willow thickets and small woodlots. And while the birds weren't plentiful, we managed some, shooting over Risky's points, always pretty, the coveys breaking from cover and fanning across Alberta wheatlands before disappearing like winged ghosts.

I said: "I don't know if we can bring in many birds with just a couple of dozen decoys."

Willy boy: "Maybe not."

Sage was switched on now, hypersensitive to everything around him, as if through the stubble he lay in he were receiving transmittals that the birds' lift-off was imminent, that the cacophonous swirl of feathers above the lake that forms in advance of the morning feeding exodus was about to appear.

"There it is," Willy boy said a moment later. "They'll be coming out now."

If you are a hunter of geese and you know what you're doing you have options. You can scout the birds the night before while they feed in stubble or plowing, and you can be at that spot the next morning, your decoy spread fully pitched, hoping the birds will return. But in goose hunting, as in life generally, what you expect to occur rarely does. So you don't outright assume the birds will be there the next morning.

"Remember, Willy boy," I said, "we're looking for the oddballs, the loners and skeptics among the flock who say the hell with safety in numbers."

Willy boy rose from the stubble and positioned himself more alertly behind our makeshift blind. He tipped over his now-empty coffee cup. He jacked a shell into the chamber of his Remington.

Then he said: "Gotcha."

Immediately following which, and almost simultaneously with the thunderous rising of birds from the not-too-distant lake, a loud bell rang out from the nearby Hutterite colony, signaling, Willy boy and I assumed, that breakfast there was either beginning or ending and that the day's work would soon be at hand. It was work that may have taken one of the young boys atop a colony silo. From this vantage point he could have seen our decoys, behind which Willy boy and Sage and I awaited the coming of the now-flighted tens of thousands of birds whose landing gear was up, a new day begun.

"A couple out front."

"I see 'em."

Since our days in college, when what we hunted we ate that night, Willy boy and I have shared blinds like these. So when the geese started coming off the lake, some headed in our direction, there was no need for communication. Willy boy watched. I watched. Sage watched. Each of us dismissed, first, the pair of honkers that flared from our decoys prematurely, then the passing of a couple of hundred speckled-bellies that flew too high, then scores and scores of others, all cruising at safe altitudes.

But before long a stranger of the kind Willy boy and I sought appeared on the near horizon, a big Canada bearing down on our spread from the right side, tangentially. Seeing this, Willy boy went to his call, head down. Then I joined in, mine offering a deeper, almost contralto counterpoint to his plaintive *honk, honk*. Carlos Santana at the Fillmore it wasn't, but to the appreciative ear it was a pretty sound.

Then the goose did the unexpected, diverting its apparent flight plan over our decoys to one that would bring it alongside our blind, perhaps out of range. In response, Willy boy embellished his call with a frantic edge, the wind still coming hard across the prairie, but the morning cold long since forgotten.

When the goose returned Willy's call, I peeked up.

The bird was nearly above us.

I dropped my call and signaled with my thumb to Willy boy that the goose was topside.

Seconds later, we both came up, shouldering our guns.

Then we watched as the bird folded and fell 50 yards distant.

22

"Sage," I said, and the big black Lab bounded across the stubble, narrowed eyes focused on the point of impact, the dog not noticing as behind him Willy boy and I disappeared once again into our blind. With fresh coffee poured and Willy boy's call alternating with mine, we awaited the arrival of still more birds from the lake in the middle distance.

Willy's Cabin

Willy and I go back a long time if you count the fishing trip to Kabetogama, the hunts in west-central Minnesota, and the time we got kicked out of Breckenridge, Colorado, on a night so cold I had to wake him up every hour or so to start the car and run the heater.

I was scrunched up in the back seat, half in and half out of a too-small sleeping bag, and Willy was in the front seat near the heater, which was fine for him but not for me. When the cold got to be too much, I yelled Willy to start the engine, and then I punched the back of the seat. Willy would crank up his old Chevelle six-cylinder stick and then fall asleep again, so 15 minutes later I would yell to Willy to shut off the engine. By doing so I reckon he saved our lives more than one time.

We were in the mountains looking for work, or so we had convinced ourselves. It was Willy's car that we drove, slept, and ate in. For good measure we were pulling a trailer and in it rode my Harley Davidson, which we figured would come in handy if by chance we got work at separate job sites. The trailer was ours courtesy of a rental outfit that by some mistake or miscalculation of theirs employed a friend of ours. "If you get out to Colorado and don't need it any more, just push it off a cliff," he said as we hooked it up and drove off in the direction of the setting sun.

I figured it would take only one or two more blasts from the heater before dawn arrived, but in keeping with the theme of the trip the cops came first. One of them rapped on the window and proceeded to tell us how we were about as welcome in Breckenridge as a snowless winter and as a consequence we should get on down the road pronto, which is what we did. A day or two later we gave up on Colorado, bought four cases of Coors, and headed back to Minnesota.

I was thinking about this one day when fall was in the air somewhat earlier than expected, and I decided to throw a fishing rod, tackle box, shotgun, two boxes of shells, two training dummies, a whistle, and my two dogs into the car and head west to Willmar for a day in the country with Willy and Jake, Willy's new black Lab.

I turned off 494 and onto Highway 12, zipped past Wayzata, and wound through Long Lake. The air was chilled enough to keep the windows up. The morning rain was still falling. By the time the dogs had settled down and stopped licking the nape of my neck and the scenery in the rearview mirror had changed from concrete gray to farmland green, I was feeling good—feeling good because I have more country in me than city and more autumn in me than summer. Besides which, I was going to see Willy and Jake.

Willy is like a lot of my friends in that he lives in a small town, and I am not telling him anything new when I say that he is better off for it. I say this again as he shows me through his house, which is decorated as it should be, with enough Harvey Dunne prints to please the eye and enough pictures of ducks and geese to stir the imagination.

We transferred my stuff to Willy's Bronco and headed toward Renville and beyond to the Minnesota River valley where Willy, one of his brothers, and his dad own 80 acres of hunting land. The land is prime. This year one of their four sloughs is almost dry, but in a good year all of them hold ducks. The land also is excellent for deer, and in each of the recent years the Smith family has taken at least one.

Before walking to Willy's A-frame cabin, we take the gun, my dogs, and the practice dummies to the best duck spot on the land. From a blind hidden in the bulrushes near shore we throw the dummies again and again for the dogs. Of course the slough stinks with the smell of algae, and soon the dogs stink too and they love it. I never will cease to be amazed at a dog's almost insatiable desire to stink in this manner. And I mean really stink.

Willy's cabin sits on a substantial granite outcropping and overlooks another slough, this one too thick with rushes and too shy of water to hunt. We enter the cabin and Willy says now it's Miller time but quickly adds that we have forgotten the beer, and I am thinking this must be a sign of something. When Willy and I were in school at Morris this never would have occurred; at least we would have remembered the elixir that has won the hearts of more than one collegian: Ripple wine.

Feeling betrayed by our forgetfulness, Willy offers to make some tea and begins scrounging through the cabinets. Lo and behold if he doesn't come across an unopened pint of Yukon Jack, a liquor that has always won my heart for its taste, its name, and for the fact that its mother company has seen fit to use the prose and poetry of Robert Service in its advertisements. I figure if the stuff is good enough to invoke the wisdom of Robert Service it is, by damn, good enough for me.

Now many people may not see this as a good time, but to me they come no better. What more could one ask? The city is far enough away to forget and the country is close enough to soak up. What's more my dogs are nearby and because they stink real good they're happy too.

As the dogs fall asleep the conversation turns to hunting and anti-hunters and pro-hunters. Willy allows as how he can't understand why some people are so much against hunting and I agree, saying that it was second nature in my family and that most of my friends hunt as well. Willy agrees but says the guys who are slobs about hunting and who brag about how much they kill are no better really. This struck me as a good point and I told him so.

Later that evening, after we walked around the 80 acres, after we drove back to Willmar, and after I reloaded my car, I left for the Twin Cities. This is a drive I have made from just about every angle possible, from north, south, east, and west, and from all directions in between, and I have never liked it. It occurs to me that this is because in cities there are too many unnatural and unpredictable stimuli that demand responses that all too often are also unnatural and unpredictable.

As I am thinking about this the city lights turn night into day and awaken the dogs, and they begin pacing nervously.

Alaska for Ducks

If you worked on the oil rigs near Prudhoe Bay, Alaska, you would, on days off, likely seek refuge in Fairbanks, where Willy and I once found ourselves with a couple of friends from Minnesota. Having more money than time, you would, like many roughnecks, fly commercially or perhaps charter a small plane, arriving in Fairbanks intent on securing your share of fun.

Some roughnecks spend a portion of their time in Fairbanks at strip joints, where women, young and middle-aged alike, work after responding to advertisements, some in Lower 48 newspapers. The advertisements promise big money, $800 a week in some cases, for female "dancers," a term loosely employed. And women do come, some from Oregon, others from Florida, and upon arrival are housed in nearby bunks and given names such as "Ecstasy" and "Star." On weekday nights they join as many as 45 other dancers working clubs not much bigger than double-wide mobile homes, their names flashing on computer screens when they take the stage.

Now if you were a duck hunter and not a roughneck and had spent the last week on what is essentially an 800-square-mile Alaskan marsh called Minto Flats, housed in a 12-by-16-foot shack, eating generous portions of duck and geese and fish, but without the luxury of a shower, you might, upon returning to Fairbanks, and upon taking a shower, find yourself shoulder to shoulder in a strip joint with the roughnecks.

Then again you might not.

Instead you might be satisfied to lie on your motel bed, reviewing occurrences of the past week, thinking of the thousands of ducks you had seen and the sound of sandhill cranes, and the evenings spent sitting on the small porch of the shack, eating hors d'oeuvres and sipping Yukon Jack, awaiting dinner while watching the warm sun go gently into the night.

Lying on your Fairbanks motel bed you would also recall how the float-equipped Cessna 185 carried you 45 minutes from Fairbanks, across mountains and through cloud banks before dipping over the flats, scattering ducks, and how the plane, piloted by a man named Bob Elliott, landed on the muddy flats and taxied to your tiny shack, which was separated from the water by a makeshift foundation of cement blocks piled five high.

Like an oversized outhouse on stilts, the shack, replete with canvas top, rose preposterously from the Minto Flats, appearing as if from nowhere, standing alone in the marsh, flanked only by two small boats with two equally small outboard motors.

Crude though it was, the shack provided refuge from the water below and rain above. The shack was also warm, except at night when the fire in the wood stove routinely expired, allowing outside cold to filter through the plywood walls like so much unwelcome music.

In a week on the Minto Flats, alone except for the occasional drone of an airplane overhead or the infrequent passing of a jet boat, this was the Alaska we—Bruce Bliel, Willy Smith, Jeff Finden, and I—knew.

The duck hunters among you will want to know what waterfowl we saw, and I can say we saw in interior Alaska what we see in Minnesota: mallards, wigeon, bluebills, blue-winged teal, green-winged teal, shovelers, speckled-belly geese, Canada geese, buffleheads, goldeneyes, canvasback, pintails, redheads, and ruddy ducks.

Duck hunters will also want to know what the hunting was like, inasmuch as in duck hunting there is pass shooting, decoy shooting,

29

jump shooting, and variations and combinations thereof.

What we had in Alaska, largely, was pass shooting. There was some decoying of ducks but, unlike in Minnesota, it was marginal. Always we had decoys placed before us, but rarely did they earn anything more than passing glances from the birds, which were not easily fooled. This was, after all, their home, where they had returned last spring, where they had nested and reared their young, where they had flown all summer. To them a few dozen decoys were just so much litter on the water.

This was our daily schedule.

Come morning, at 4:30 we would arise, unzipping ourselves from sleeping bags and stepping uneasily atop the cold wooden floor, careful not to trip over boots or guns or shells or jackets or any of the other paraphernalia scattered about the shack. Then one of us would scratch a match against the wall or floor and ignite a kerosene lantern, whose muted light provided visibility but not much noise. The portable cots on which we slept were then stacked atop one another, and the process of donning long underwear, canvas pants, and rainwear was undertaken, each of us vying for position amid the cramped quarters.

The early breakfast, as we called it, consisted only of oatmeal with brown sugar and raisins, fried bread, orange juice, and a form of hot water we called coffee. When this was consumed, we filled two thermos bottles with the coffee, grabbed two candy bars apiece, and stepped into the waiting darkness.

At our disposal were two boats, one a 14-foot john, the other a pointed-bow aluminum job that, if you pulled the proper pins, would fold up like a squeaky accordion. Both were powered by 2-horsepower outboard motors, which propelled the boats only slowly, allowing us sufficient time to consume even more coffee en route to hunting spots.

We hunted in twos, changing partners daily, sometimes leaving the shack in different directions as each set of hunters sought new and better hunting. On the first days our luck was only fair. It took time to develop an understanding of the birds, where they liked to fly, where they didn't like to fly, and the times at which our chances were best to intercept them.

We finally decided it did no good to establish decoy spreads in small bays or marshes and lie in ambush until birds arrived. For better shooting we took to placing decoys along small rivers that connected the bigger lakes and marshes of the Minto Flats. This allowed greater opportunities at the birds, because most of the ducks in the air flew along these waterways.

When the morning hunt was ended at nine or ten, we would pick up the decoys and *putt-putt-putt* back to the shack, gut and hang the birds, and set about the business of cooking a breakfast of French toast and eggs and potatoes.

Later, arising in the early afternoon from a nap, we would gather on the porch and discuss issues of world import while Willy assembled a plate of sardines, crackers, and cheese and Bruce oversaw the pouring of communion-sized portions of Yukon Jack, all while Jeff, bent over a two-burner gas stove, was busy concocting stews of ducks or geese and rice, hearty stuff worthy even of Robert Service.

By 6:00 P.M., we were hunting again, spending the last three hours of daylight watching plastic ducks bob on the waves of the Minto Flats.

If we were to imagine ourselves not atop Minto Flats but above it, higher than a duck can fly, higher even than the flight of the sandhill cranes that nest each summer in the Soviet Union before crossing the Bering Sea and migrating south in the fall, we would have a vantage point from which we could appreciate the contrasts of Alaska. This is what we would see.

Below, on the flats, Willy, Jeff, Bruce, and I go about our daily business, arising early and hunting late.

To the north and west, on the Arctic coast of Alaska, Eskimos prepare for hunts of their own, for shots at migrating caribou, at polar bears and at walrus, whose ivory tusks are later sold, piece by piece, in

31

the gift shops of Fairbanks and Anchorage and Juneau, the deals sealed with Visa or MasterCard.

We see also, to the east, in Fairbanks, a single-engine plane lifting into the air, its pilot, a special agent of the U.S. Fish and Wildlife Service, alone in the cockpit as he guides the plane west and north, beginning a patrol of an area roughly the equivalent to that bounded in the Lower 48 by Maine, Florida, and Ohio.

"I spend a lot of time with the Eskimos, helping them understand regulations governing the taking of polar bears, walrus, and other game," the agent, Dan Mayer, will tell you. "Hunting is their life. They're very interested in what I have to say."

The special agent will also tell you he spends a like amount of time enforcing Alaskan games laws as interpreted by other Alaskans, resident of, say, Fairbanks, some of whom guide powerful jet boats up the Tanana River to the Minto Flats, a three-hour trip, and use the boats to frighten ducks into flight. They then shoot the birds from the moving boats, a practice as illegal as it is unsportsmanlike, but then everything has its dark side.

Now, from our vantage point above the flats, we see four of these Fairbanks residents, all men, huddled around a small fire outside the 12-by-16-foot shack. But these are fishermen, not hunters, anglers who flew to the flats looking for a day of northern pike fishing, but who fell victim to the cold autumn rains of Alaska and hope now only to stay marginally warm until their plane returns to fly them again to Fairbanks.

And the plane does return. But weather across the mountains is bad and the pilot will make but one flight to Fairbanks, not the two needed to transport all four anglers. So one man, a bearded, heavy-set tough-talker, must remain overnight, sleeping on the floor of the shack next to the wood stove.

Bruce, Willy, Jeff, and I return from hunting that evening, and after we remove wet clothes and make a fresh pot of coffee, the bearded, heavy-set tough-talker tells us about himself.

"Like a lot of people who live here, I was stationed in Alaska in the service. I'm from Georgia, but after I got out of the Army there was nothing there for me. So I came back up here. I'm a mechanic. I got a job in a garage.

"Now I own a garage, but things are soft up here right now. Everybody's waiting for the next big boom when they start building the gas line. A lot of people made a lot of money when the pipeline was built. I mean a lot of money. But it's gone now. Everybody blew it. Drank it up, or whatever.

"My friends and me, we get out quite a bit. Like today. It was a lark, more or less, to fly over here and fish. Last week we went up north for caribou and moose. We got five caribou and two moose, which was about average. It's a long winter, you know."

I say: "Too bad you're stuck here tonight, wet and cold. If you had gotten home, you could have cleaned up and been sitting in front of a warm fireplace with your wife watching TV."

"Ya," says the bearded, heavy-set tough-talker, "or in some bar."

Three days later Bob Elliott's plane appears over the mountains. Again the weather is not good, but Elliott, a Fairbanks native who has flown the Alaskan bush for more than two decades without an accident, gets us out.

In Fairbanks, we are shuttled to a motel, where a sign in the lobby reads: Patrons must check guns and knives before entering bar.

Later, an aging cab driver, who had abandoned Brooklyn for Fairbanks hoping for a piece of the Alaskan action, ferries us first to a pizza place and then, after dropping one of our party at the motel, proceeds to the aforementioned strip joint, describing it in advance not as such but, rather, as a tavern roughly akin to the one portrayed in the television show "Cheers."

"Tell Paul I said you were OK," the cabbie mutters as he drops us off.

"Yo," comes the response.

Then, embracing a faint sense of vertigo, we step lightly toward the tavern door, noticing only momentarily that the unmarked establishment is nearly encircled by a cyclone fence.

Autumn in Ely

Autumn came sooner to Alaska than Minnesota, but when it came to Minnesota, it came to Ely first. At sun-up on White Iron Lake, not far outside Ely, the mercury in a thermometer nailed to an old tree rested at 46 degrees Fahrenheit, surely an indication not only of what was no longer to be but of what was to come.

All of which made me quite content, and a little nervous. On mornings such as these I am like a huge antenna, and the signals I receive are mixed. Arriving on one wavelength is considerable relief that summer has ended, and with it the idleness of thought and action that constant temperatures and blue skies often produce. On another wavelength, the onset of autumn brings thoughts of mortality, thoughts that bear little comfort unless one has all of one's loose ends tied in neat little knots, which I don't.

But such are the dilemmas of the season, and as I sat in a glassed porch high on a cliff overlooking White Iron Lake, a cup of coffee in one hand, my chin in the other, I gave considerable thought to details in need of tending. There was a quick mental inventory of winter clothing: of boots to mend and of wool socks to purchase. So too were there thoughts of my truck, of its need for new and bigger tires, also minor body work, a tune-up, and radiator back-flush. Also, the basement freezer is in need of cleaning in preparation for the fish and game that will be gathered this fall.

The gathering of food is for me a proper ceremony of autumn, and one that contributes not only to nutritional needs but to psychological ones as well. Others may acquire their meat in cellophane packages bearing blue numbers, but I opt, instead, to make my acquisitions in more memorable manners, preferably those involving odoriferous hunting dogs, crimson sunrises over dank marshes, and harvest moons silhouetting Farmall combines.

It was from these thoughts that I was, in effect, awakened when Bob and Dea Whitten, hosts on White Iron Lake to me and my dogs, announced that a slice of heaven was being placed on the kitchen table in the form of blueberry pancakes, the blueberries having been picked by Bob and Dea at a site not far from their home.

"This is the easy way to make blueberry pancakes," Dea said, placing what appeared to be a large flat cake on the table. "I got the recipe from the Ducks Unlimited cookbook."

No further recommendation was needed, and the four of us bellied up to the table to begin the feast, passing, in order, the pancakes, the butter, and the maple syrup. Meanwhile, outside and clearly visible stood my two dogs, Belle and Risky, together with Nemo, Bob and Dea's bear-sized black Lab. Each pressed a nose against the sliding-glass door; each wagged a tail side to side metronomically.

After breakfast there was a ride in Bob's boat—painted camouflage, of course—first along the shoreline of White Iron Lake, then through Silver Rapids, and finally into or near Farm and Garden lakes. All the while, light rain slanted from the charcoal sky, stinging our faces but feeling good, even refreshing.

Following the ride was a short walk along a long road, during which the dogs performed canine gymnastics of a kind even Jack Lalanne would admire, what with two-paw burnouts, four-paw skids, and tail-chasing pirouettes. It was as if the dogs could feel, as we did, transformation in the air, the shifting of gears from summer into fall.

Later we would walk up and down Sheridan Street, one of Ely's two main thoroughfares, purchase a wool sweater at The Spinning Wheel, and eat lunch at Our Mom's Cafe. Later still, we would visit Elizabeth Olson, wife of the late naturalist and author Sigurd Olson, and listen as Elizabeth recounted her latest exploits, including a month-long sojourn to Alaska to visit son Sig Jr. Elizabeth noted, as we had, that seasonal changes were afoot, pinpointing, while giving us a tour of her yard, summer flowers now in descent.

There was a final stop outside of Ely, this at the home of friends Bill and Martha Scott, during which we found Bill reloading shotgun shells for the upcoming hunting season. Then it was on to Eveleth, an hour to the south, where we would spend the night.

En route, on the back roads connecting Ely, Babbitt, Embarrass, and, finally, Eveleth, the skies cleared and the day became a window through which I could see mid-October. At one juncture, a lone Canada goose flew above us, preparing, it seemed, for the long flight ahead, just as all around us, moose and deer and whiskey jacks and beavers and wolves and all other forms of life were preparing.

Summer had ended.

Autumn was just up the road.

Dorothy Molter

A quiet evening in canoe country near Ely some years ago. Wind rustles the pines, waves lick the dock gently, but the mosquitoes stand firm.

Dorothy Molter walks the path, swatting the air as she goes. "I found a canoe, I found a dog, but I didn't find you," she says, the familiar smile creasing her face. "I saw you coming up the lake, but by the time I got down to the dock, you were gone."

Dorothy Molter is a legend in these parts, has been for 51 years, which is how long she's lived in the Boundary Waters. That's a long time, 51 years, long enough to earn her the title of Loneliest Woman in America, which is what the *Saturday Evening Post* labeled her a couple of decades back. Not true, of course—Dorothy's alone, not lonely—but it makes good copy.

"Have you eaten? The boys aren't back from fishing yet, and I was going to wait before I made supper, but I can get you something if you'd like."

"Just coffee, maybe," I say, "and a root beer."

When Dorothy first came to Knife Lake, the region was unknown to all but a few men who lived nearby or traversed it as fishermen, trappers, or guides. And the lumberjacks, the lumberjacks knew the area, too. It was nothing like it is today, when canoes glide up and down Knife Lake from May to October, carrying fortune seekers of one sort or another. Most want fish, many want solitude, all want a break from civilization.

Dorothy, who's from Chicago originally, first traveled these parts with her father, John C. "Cap" Molter. During the trips she became familiar with the Boundary Waters and liked them, so much so that she continued her visits during her years in nursing school, years that prepared her for a career but not for the Depression.

"Work was very scarce then," Dorothy said, sitting at the table in her summer cabin, which is more tent than cabin. "And the man who owned these islands was sick for many years, so I came up here to help out. It was better than sitting around waiting for no work to come in."

As the man aged and his condition worsened, Dorothy's responsibilities grew. There was wood to be chopped, chores to be done. And even though she was assuming a man's role in a man's wilderness, she remained a woman. And in those days women had their place.

"I used to stay in the background a lot when the other men came around," Dorothy said. "They would have their own things to talk about, and I always found something else to do until they were gone."

In 1948 the man died. There had been rough times with him before, times when Dorothy tied three dish rags to the boat house to signal planes for help, and other times when she scribbled her messages in the snow, so his death came as little surprise. Nonetheless, it upset Dorothy's life and plans, and she returned to Chicago. When she did, she was unaware her boss and friend had left her the islands, which span 10 acres and lie in the western end of Knife Lake on the Minnesota–Canada border.

Upon hearing the news, Dorothy packed her bags and headed north. This time, she returned to a home she could call her own.

At 74, despite the fact she has never married, Dorothy appears the quintessential grandmother, with her silvery white hair, her kind smile, and eyes that twinkle when she grins. She is an unassuming woman, one who freely shares her home and time with some 6,000 canoeists each summer, canoeists who tie up at her dock seeking a candy bar or a bottle of homemade root beer, both of which are priced at three for a buck. Three root beers, three candy bars, or two of one and one of another. Three for a buck.

She's a big woman, a strong woman with hands and arms of substance. Her strength, in fact, is described with some reverence by those who knew her years back, when she could cut, split, and stack wood with Bunyanesque ease. Today, she still gathers and splits wood, but the fingers are filled with arthritis and the going is slower. The chores get done, the root beer gets made, but more slowly and with a little more help than in the past.

"I've been making root beer since 1950," Dorothy says. "The planes used to bring pop up here, until the airplane ban of 1949. But after they stopped flying I still had all these bottles lying around, and I thought there ought to be something I could do with them, so I tried making root beer. At first it wasn't very good, but gradually I cracked down on the yeast, and I've been making it that way ever since."

Dorothy gets all her supplies from Ely, including the candy bars and extract, syrup, and yeast needed to make Knife Lake's favorite brew. Everything must be loaded in canoes at Moose Lake, about 18 miles northeast of Ely, for the trip back to Dorothy's. Five portages must be crossed, or, in lieu of that, the canoe or canoes must be pulled up the rapids. No matter what the choice, it's a lot of work for one person, be it a man or a woman.

"One time I was coming back from Ely," Dorothy says, "and I had so many supplies I had to make seven trips across each one of the five portages. It was just getting dark as I got to the first portage and started carrying the supplies across.

"I made six trips with no trouble, and I said to myself, 'Gee, I'm lucky I haven't met up with any bears yet.' But when I went back for my last pack, I smelled a bear's wet fur, so I hurried to get the pack across before the bear found my supplies.

"When I finally got across the portage for the last time, it was dark, so I checked off my stuff to make sure I didn't leave anything behind. I found one pack was missing.

"I didn't know what to do. I was sure I brought it over, so I made a lot of noise, trying to scare off the bear if he was nearby. After I did, I walked through the bushes, thinking that I could get the pack back if I had scared him away. I didn't find it, and I was just about to turn back to the canoe when I looked up. There, in front of me, was a huge black bear, standing on his hind legs with his mouth open.

"I was just out of his reach, but he kept reaching out with his paw and swiping at me. I didn't know what to do, so I stood it out for as long as I could, then took a slow step backward. But with every move I made, the bear let out a big growl and took a step forward. Still, I was slowly able to turn away from him and walk away.

"I don't know how long it took to get away from the bear, but it was a long time. Finally, I picked my way down to the canoe and left. That was the last portage I made that night. I pulled the canoe up all the other rapids."

Where there is root beer there must be ice to keep it cold. To get hers, Dorothy cuts it out of the lake in the winter, surrounds it with moss and sawdust, and stores it. Amazingly, it lasts all summer.

But does her work provide her with sufficient companionship?

"Oh, I don't mind the solitude," Dorothy says, pouring another cup of coffee. "Sometimes I can hardly wait for the fall. When I first came up here I only saw 15 people a month, and nobody ever stopped unless they were in trouble. Now, about 6,700 people stop here during the summer. In the spring and fall it's OK, because it's just the smaller groups. But in the summer, the big groups of kids come through and I don't like them as much.

"No, this is the only place I've ever had that I could call my own. I worked hard for it, and I'll stay here as long as I can take care of myself."

She speaks the words with assurance. But the tone belies the troubles

41

lying ahead for Dorothy, troubles that could cost her the only life she's known.

In 1978, Congress passed its most recent BWCA bill, which immediately eliminated most of the motor and snowmobile routes in the wilderness area, and provided for a five-year phaseout of the others. One of the routes being phased out runs from Moose lake, the route Dorothy uses to get her supplies. Unless some provision is made for her (and none is planned at this time), Dorothy Molter, who will then be 77 years old, will, in effect, be cut off from civilization. No more LP gas, no more candy bars, no more root beer. Just the essentials, which may or may not be enough.

"I'll have to do without a lot of things," Dorothy says. "And my sister, who's been coming up to stay with me for parts of the summer and winter, won't be able to come anymore, either. She can't paddle a canoe all the way from Moose Lake.

"And the snowmobiles won't be able to come anymore with supplies. Some of the men from Ely and Babbitt have been coming up to help with the ice in the winter, and they won't be able to do that. . . . I used to walk back to Moose Lake in the winter—it's an eight-hour walk on snowshoes—but I can't do that very much anymore.

"I just don't like this no-motors rule," Dorothy adds. "I think it's silly. There's no reason why a man in his middle years can't use a motor up here. The way they've got it now, it'll be just for the young people. Motors don't pollute any more than these big groups of kids that come up here in the summer."

With that she finishes her coffee, puts the cup on the table, and is silent, as if perplexed. Dorothy is a compassionate woman, one who has put the needs of others ahead of her own, who has helped hundreds of campers and fed scores of Forest Service crews. For her, it is difficult to understand why she is the butt of this injustice, why she should be trapped for embodying the very wilderness spirit the 1978 BWCA law represents.

There is little doubt the cards are stacked against her. Unless some provision is made for her or her representative (her grandnephew has been helping her the past five summers) to use a motor to get back to Ely for supplies, she may well be forced out of her home. Not that the Forest Service would mind. They already own her islands, having purchased them in 1967 during one of the many BWCA buy-outs that have occurred in recent decades. They've got their locks on some of her cabins as well, though by earlier agreement Dorothy is allowed to stay as long as she wishes.

"I could make it," Dorothy says, the late-night discussion nearly complete. "I've still got family in Chicago, but I usually get sick when I go there to visit. . . . I could still make it, but it would be hard."

EPILOGUE

The U.S. Forest Service developed a plan beginning about 1982 to deliver supplies to Dorothy, to provide her transportation back to Ely as needed, and to help her cut wood for heating. The Forest Service also allowed Dorothy personal use of a motor on Knife Lake, despite the federal law prohibiting others from using motors on the lake.

Dorothy Molter was found dead in her Knife Lake cabin on December 17, 1986.

Bud Grant

It's nighttime and Bud Grant, whose need for solitude is not unlike that of Dorothy Molter, is putting the big Buick through its paces, guiding it east along U.S. Highway 12, a bullet on the blacktop.

With three days on the North Dakota prairies behind us, we're headed home to Minnesota, a few sharp-tailed grouse in the cooler and two dogs, one his, one mine, asleep in the back of the station wagon.

A talk show is on the radio. The subject is the Minnesota Vikings. It's Thursday night and the Vikings play the Lions in Detroit on Sunday, a fact of considerable importance to most who call.

"So what about this Tommy Kramer? Is he just rusty or what?" asks one.

A curious phenomenon, this. As the team's head coach for 17 years, Bud and the Vikings are close. Though no longer coaching, he remains a consultant and is knowledgeable about the team, its players, its system. The two are . . . well, family, and here is Bud, driving along U.S. Highway 12, bisecting tiny burgs like Ortonville, Danvers, DeGraff, and Murdock, listening while people talk about his family.

We drive over a slight rise and find a little old lady putt-putt-putting down the blacktop, speedometer registering about 40. Bud eases the Buick into the passing lane and kicks the accelerator to the floor, force-feeding the big V-8. As he does, a long-nose Kenworth crests the next rise, westbound, its headlights staring at us, big as sin.

I want to say, "Hesitate and we're history."

But I say nothing.

A couple of years back, Bud and I were flying out of Seattle. We were in a small jet and when the tower gave us the OK, the pilot shoved the throttles forward, hurtling us down the runway. But the nose wheel had accidentally been turned backward, and the plane suddenly veered right, forcing the pilot to hit the brakes, aborting the takeoff.

I wanted to say something then, too.

But Bud didn't say anything.

So I didn't say anything.

Finally, Bud pulls into the right lane, slightly ahead of the little old lady, and very slightly ahead of the Kenworth.

Into the night we go.

Radio playing, dogs sleeping, frozen sharptails in the cooler.

I'll tell you this about Bud Grant: He's got a no-nonsense Model 50 Winchester ("Like most other things that work well, they aren't made anymore"), a no-nonsense black Lab, and an uncanny ability to mispronounce my dog's name.

"You take Frisky and walk the ridge," he would say in Dakota. "I'll take Molly and walk the bottom."

"It's Risky, not Frisky. Do I look like a guy who'd name a dog Frisky?"

"So what kind of name is Risky?"

"Look. Call my dog Risky and I'll call your dog Molly. Otherwise, I'll call her Polly."

I'll tell you another thing about Bud Grant: Except while hunting, he doesn't shoot a gun much. Claims he's never broken a clay target in his 57 years, but he's a good shot.

"I never want to become too good a shooter," he says. "When I put the gun up, I want to be surprised. What fun is it to know you'll hit everything you shoot? There has to be some suspense.

"Besides, it's good that some birds get away."

This North Dakota thing was Bud's idea. Two years ago, when the NFL was shut down by a players' strike, he drove to an area south and west of Bismarck—the same prairies we hunted this year—and made his first try at North Dakota sharptails.

By night, he slept in an abandoned farmhouse. By day, he and his dog hunted birds.

"When the players walked out, I looked around to see what seasons were open. And what was open was North Dakota grouse."

He also hunted Saskatchewan, Manitoba, South Dakota, Minnesota, and Wisconsin during the strike.

"We'd find out on Thursday whether the players were going to report for Sunday's game. If they weren't, I had until Sunday night to hunt."

Whether or not the players' strike and the hunting it allowed him prompted Bud to think anew about the advantages of retirement is unknown. He had hunted a lot before, around Winnipeg as well as in Minnesota, so he was aware of what he was missing.

"I knew what was out there," he said. "There were no surprises."

Still, not many years ago, when a friend and I were hunting a marsh near the Twin Cities, Bud rowed his boat over to ours. It was early and ducks were still flying, but Bud was headed to the office.

"You guys with all the time," he said. "It must be nice."

When Bud and I left the Twin Cities, we drove by the Vikings' Eden Prairie offices.

"This is a first," Bud said, meaning that, for the first time since before he was a college kid at the University of Minnesota, he was beginning an autumn week the way it should begin—by leaving the Twin Cities.

To him what lay behind the brick walls at the Vikings' offices was all too familiar: Coaches were reviewing films of the team's victory over Atlanta, trying to determine what went right and what went wrong;

players were working out, getting patched up, or watching game film; and everyone, particularly the coaches, was squeezed for time.

"Monday, Tuesday, and Wednesday are a coach's busiest days," Bud said.

"Monday, you review Sunday's game, trying to get whatever value you can from it. You talk about the could-have-beens and the should-have-beens, then put it behind you. Monday evening, you watch films of the next opponent.

"On Tuesday, the players are off, but the coaches put their game plan together for the next Sunday.

"And on Wednesday, the plan is put to paper, mimeographed, and given to the players.

"It's a very structured, very one-dimensional life. I lived nearby, so I could go home for supper, then come back and work until ten or eleven. But most coaches ate right in the office.

"Some weeks were tougher, some easier. How long it took is how long you stayed."

Much of western North Dakota is good sharptail country. The ranch we hunted was owned by Bud's friends Dave and Molly Ten Broek. It was 10:00 A.M. each day before we loaded our guns and started walking ravines and draws. Nearly every piece of land we walked held at least some birds, frequently as many as two or three coveys.

We used both a Lab and a setter, but the birds didn't hold very well for either. Perhaps it was because rain hadn't fallen in North Dakota since June, making the prairies brittle and, to sharptails, quite noisy. Whatever the reason, the birds were edgy.

One time, we walked a fairly steep ravine. Shortly after we began, a covey flushed high and to my right. I shot, dropping two. Then Risky and I climbed out of the ravine, allowing Bud and Molly to continue the push.

Occasionally, a bird rose ahead of them, escaping out of range. But

Molly was in hot pursuit of those that remained, flushing one covey, then another. Bud shouldered the Model 50, dropping two birds. Continuing, he flushed maybe 15 more before firing a third time to fill his daily limit.

It was hunting as hunting should be, with sufficient physical exertion to make it demanding, and enough birds to make it exciting.

Somehow, Bud handled the pressure.

One night, after eating a ranch-sized meal of sharptails, Dave, Molly, Bud, and I sat in the Ten Broeks' living room talking dogs, birds, cattle, and other items of importance.

I excused myself to call home. When I returned, I told Bud the Vikings had traded Steve Dils to Los Angeles.

Bud said, "They did, huh?"

Then we talked dogs, birds, cattle, and other items of importance.

Deer Camp

In Wisconsin, as in North Dakota and other states, hunting camps serve as autumn bases of operation for families and friends. In cabins big and small, hunters, men and boys mostly, gather to renew friendships and to hunt. In the process, boys mature and men evolve.

The cadence and attitude of camps vary. In some, emphasis is placed on the hunt, on how many birds or deer fall to the guns. Social concerns dominate others. Most depend on both. Without at least a chance of taking game, the gathering would be vacuous, without purpose; but so, too, the camp without friends or family.

A deer-hunting camp not far from Barronett in northwestern Wisconsin is typical of many. It is owned by Norb Berg of Mendota Heights, Minnesota, but in a larger sense it is the property of Berg and his four brothers, all of whom live in Wisconsin: Father Don of Wausau, a Catholic priest; Tom of Stevens Point; Marv of Merrill; and Dave of Edgar.

The Bergs grew up in Edgar, a small town in central Wisconsin, part of a family that also included three sisters. Oddly, neither their father nor mother hunted. Hunting was something the boys picked up individually or in pairs.

For the last dozen years or so, since the time the Barronett cabin was purchased, the Bergs, their sons, and a handful of friends have hunted deer together here.

The first hunts were not very productive. The odd deer was taken, but the area herd was small and sightings few. In response, habitat improvement projects were begun. Tracts of land were cleared by the Bergs and other landowners, and by the state.

Says Norb: "To increase the size of the herd, we cleared off a '40.' Gerry Murphy, my neighbor, cleared some land, too. It made quite a difference, and in a relatively short time. In the years since, we've logged a little land at a time. It's worked quite well."

Over the years, a camp ritual has evolved. On Friday night before opening day, the Berg clan and a few friends gather at Spanky's, a supper club in Barronett, a tiny town straddling U.S. Highway 63 just north of Cumberland. There, toasts precede dinner, which precedes a general review of who will be on which deer stand come sunrise, which precedes a series of exaggerated recollections about past seasons.

Friends join in the merriment. Elmer Severson, of rural Barronett, a part-time farmer whose physical appearance approximates that of a down-sized Paul Bunyan, is a participant. Elmer, it seems, is always happy. Also present are Bob Kolzow of nearby Cumberland, his wife, Linda, and daughter, Karen.

On Friday night this year, Dave, an amateur guitarist, singer, and songwriter, provided the music at Spanky's. This was a rare undertaking. Discounting the animated conversation of Don the bartender, Spanky's doesn't usually offer live entertainment. But the establishment's patrons, easy-going by nature and homespun in their humor, took the music in stride: They danced until the joint closed.

"That's the first time another guy has ever touched my butt," said one dancer, a man of about 60, who had fallen into another man during a complicated pirouette maneuver.

What brings hunters back to the same deer camp year after year is in many ways indefinable. Intangible.

"I think we've actually got more deer near home in Edgar," says Dave. "But hunting there would be different for my sons and me. We wouldn't have the camaraderie or the romanticism of getting away for a while. It would just be different and not as satisfying."

Adds Marv: "Hunting here is the highlight of the year. It has so many elements. There's the social aspect. The 'back-to-nature' aspect. And, of course, the hunting. A major portion of the anticipation is looking forward to being here with my brothers and nephews."

Just before 6:30 A.M. opening day, a dozen hunters scattered from the Berg cabin, each headed in a different direction for a preselected tree stand. Hunting were Norb, Tom, Marv, and Dave; Norb's sons Kevin, Mitch, and Tony; Tom's son, Mike; Dave's sons Ken and Mark; Phil Bifulk, a family friend from Mendota Heights; and me. Gerry Murphy, of Mendota Heights, hunted from his cabin in the same general area. Elmer Severson did likewise.

The elder Bergs are proud that each member of the younger generation can be trusted to hunt and return safely to the cabin. Watching the boys mature over the past ten years, they say, has provided infinitely more pleasure than all the deer taken during the time.

"I guess every hunter hopes his kids will grow up to be hunters," Dave says. "In a way, getting them involved in hunting parallels how a parent prepares a son or daughter for life. You teach them to do certain things; you help them learn how to do things for themselves. Then, at some point, you send them out on their own."

Norb agrees: "Learning to hunt alone is a process of becoming independent. Knowing how to start a fire with one match, knowing how to use a compass, how to use a gun, all are important, and the process by which these things are learned can be applied to other parts of their lives.

"I also think it's important that they learn from their dads and uncles. When they see people they respect as mature and conscientious being very careful about the way they handle guns and about the way they respect the woods and some of the things that can happen while hunting, they learn there's nothing sissy about being careful, about being

51

concerned for one's safety and for the safety of people around them."

The process of becoming a deer hunter is one of skill acquisition, yes, but also one of attitude development. With young hunters, killing a deer is often regarded as the lone objective of the hunt. The need for action, particularly in the company of others the same age, is obvious and understandable.

But the astute among hunters evolve beyond this point, appreciating, as they do, the hunt's more subtle qualities. Increased understanding and knowledge of the prey spawns increased respect, and, in the end, squeezing the trigger becomes not so much a goal as a recognition that a series of events, some within the hunter's control, some not, have fallen into place. Firing the rifle becomes more conclusion than climax, an end to what has provided the pleasure.

Marv is one of the hardest hunters in camp. He routinely leaves the cabin before dawn and doesn't return until after dark.

"As much as I like to get a deer," he says, "it's very unimportant that I do. I just like to hunt."

Examples like these are invaluable to young hunters and are nurtured as much as possible by the elder Bergs.

Mike, Tom's youngest boy, has yet to get a deer. Tom hopes his son handles it properly.

"I don't want him to get discouraged. I hope he doesn't go out just to go out to see if he can get a deer. I want him to enjoy it."

By nightfall on opening day, only one deer has been taken, a nine-pointer. Dave's oldest son, Ken, was the lucky hunter. He had shot does before. This was his first buck.

As hunters filtered back to the cabin, Sorels and blaze orange coats were removed and an informal meeting was convened around the kitchen table. Present in addition to those staying at the Berg cabin were Gerry and Elmer (who had taken a buck that morning), and the Kolzows, who came bearing three trays of freshly baked rolls. None of the Kolzows hunts.

"You see much?" asked Norb of the group.

"No," was the answer, almost to a man.

"How about you, Phil?"

Phil, whose stand features a wood-burning stove and a television, has been known to nod off occasionally under the guise of hunting.

Said Phil, smiling: "No, nothing."

"Tomorrow will be different. Tomorrow we're going to drive a buck right by your nose."

"Thanks a lot," said Phil. "But it'll still be a 40-yard shot."

Hors d'oeuvres were passed around the table. It was time for success tales of the day. Elmer was first.

"I took one shot at my buck, but I missed," he said. "Then my gun jammed, and the deer disappeared. When I got the gun fixed, I looked up, but I couldn't see anything. A couple of minutes later the deer came back and walked right up to me, like it was curious or something. I couldn't believe it."

Ken, who hunts with a slug gun, followed.

"The deer was bedded down near my stand when the sun came up," he said. "A short while later, a doe walked by and the buck stood up. I hit him with my first shot. When he ran, I fired four more times but missed. I found him lying dead about 100 yards away."

Father Don, the priest and eldest Berg brother, has participated in the hunts since their inception. In the initial years he joined his brothers and nephews afield, but no longer.

"He likes to come up and involve himself in the gathering," says Tom. "He likes to play cards, and he likes to see everyone. We're his family."

Father Don can be expected to arrive Sunday afternoon of opening weekend. By then he has finished with his parish obligations in Wausau and is ready to begin his respite.

But like a busman's holiday, it is not without obligations. Each year on Sunday night, Father Don offers Mass—not at a church but at a cabin in northwestern Wisconsin, not to men and women in formal dress but to his long-underwear–clad brothers and nephews.

Dave, the guitarist and singer, is the featured soloist of the event, but there are singing opportunities aplenty for the others. Some songs are sentimental; others border on rousing. Regardless, the songs serve the common purpose of unification.

"The kids aren't particularly religious," Norb says, "but they've often said this is their special Mass of the year. They like this one the best."

By mid-afternoon Monday, the group begins to disperse. Father Don, Norb, and Marv stay, but the others return home, another deer opener come and gone.

Memories of what occurred during the three days remain with the participants throughout the year.

With one exception: Often forgotten is the total number of deer killed.

Education of an
Elk Hunter

Inexperienced riders have difficulty distinguishing horses in the dark. Shapes and markings aside, the animals assume a rather universal appearance, particularly at 5:30 A.M. Looking for clues, I walked from horse to horse, running a flashlight up one leg and down another. "Lucky, that you?"

I found him tied to a small tree. I smoothed two blankets across his back and tossed up the saddle. He stared straight ahead, right rear leg lifted and bent, only the front of his shoe touching the ground. Warm breath spiraled upward from his nostrils and disappeared. I drew tight the cinch and scratched him behind the ears. "Here we go again." Nineteen degrees and a couple of inches of snow.

We were camped at 9,500 feet in a canyon in the San Juan range not far from Durango in southwest Colorado. For me it was the seventh and last complete day of hunting and so far no elk.

Inside the mess tent, Grover, the cook, was bent over a couple of dozen pieces of French toast. The wood-burning cook stove was in high gear, so too the heating stove, atop which sat a pot of coffee. Hanging from the ridgepole were four Coleman lanterns. Heat. Light. Food. Coffee. The morning was off to an impressive start.

I entered the tent. John Zink, the 67-year-old camp patriarch, was perched on a chair carved from a tree stump, tying a boot lace.

I said: "Today's the day."

"If you don't say anything else, I'll agree with you," John said.

Eight other hunters were also in camp, most of them already eating. Jess. Martha. Jim. Mark. Morris. Wayne. Steve. Jack. None had taken an elk. As luck goes, the gauge had been teetering near empty.

In a corner, a portable cassette player provided background music. The sweet country croonings of Emmy Lou Harris. What could be better? I smothered my French toast with hot syrup, poured a cup of coffee, and sat next to Jess, a 65-year-old Oklahoman, six feet four inches tall with a wooden leg.

I said: "Jess, I'd like to hear that 300 H&H echo across a canyon today."

"If I shoot, you'll know it. No mistakin' the sound of that gun."

With respect to shooting, there had been little. Martha, Jess's wife, had had a shot, but it was marginal and a clean miss. Jim had passed on a small spike bull. And I had had a shot at a spike my first day in camp. One hundred sixty yards and a 50-degree descent. Conjecture had it that I shot over him, with the elk stepping under the bullet as he angled down and away, moving in a businesslike fashion between two spruce stands.

It was my first shot at an elk, though I had hunted the animal briefly a few years back in northern Idaho. That hunt was unguided and plagued by rain, but a friend managed a spike. After dressing and boning the animal we headed back to camp. I remember tumbling down a muddy hillside, rifle in hand and 140 pounds of meat strapped to my back. I thought: If I'm going to die packing out an elk, I'd rather I be the one who shot it.

This Colorado hunt was different. It was a November affair, with cold and some snow, though not enough of the latter. We had taken five or six inches earlier in the week, but a foot or two more would have put us at an advantage. Bulls would be easier to track as they traveled from the spruce stands where they hide to the aspen stands where they feed. They would also be more visible, their brown and tan coats obvious against the snow, even from great distances.

I finished breakfast, made a sandwich for lunch, and walked to my sleeping tent, where I loaded the .270. Four cartridges in the clip but the chamber empty, the better to protect myself and my horse. If you have ridden a horse in the mountains without benefit of trails you know what I mean.

I found Lucky, deposited my gun in the scabbard attached to the saddle, and, with the others, led the horse up the darkened creek bed, away from camp.

I said: "Today's the day."

Some say elk hunting is a masochistic exercise, and this gets my vote. At 10,000 feet, the air is thin, the mountains steep, and the elk wary.

Of course a few hunters score on luck alone. The week before five bulls were taken by eight hunters. The majority were shot at less than 75 yards; one or two were felled broadside, standing still.

I would not be that lucky, I knew, though I had given such fantasies considerable air time while daydreaming. I would visualize myself back at camp, nightfall upon us and beer in hand: "I got off my horse to tighten the cinch and I happened to turn around. There was a five-point bull not 30 yards away! I tell you, I never had such luck! It happened just like in the outdoor magazines!"

But it would never occur. I was in a run of miserable luck and any shot I would get would be of the kind I already had—difficult. A Cree Indian once told me of similar problems. For three years straight he had picked the wrong hunting spots, and for as long he had hunted with little success.

"Finally I went to our chief and asked him why this was happening to me. He said if I waited long enough my fortunes would change. He said I should not take the blame for bad luck or the credit for good luck. In time, both go away."

So here I was seven days into the hunt, with no elk, riding a horse

57

whose name belied my recent track record, relying on the hearsay wisdom of an unknown Cree chief.

Across the darkened eastern sky the rising sun bled a muted crimson hue. Snow was falling to the west, the weather source. I placed my left foot in the stirrup and climbed aboard. As I did, Ed Zink, John's 36-year-old son and owner of the camp, pulled his horse alongside mine. Like me, he wore heavy wool pants, a down coat, and Sorels.

"We'll ride quite a ways this morning," Ed said, his horse spinning and snorting as he spoke. "You, Morris, Wayne, and I will post on a ridge. Steve and his crew will swing through the canyon below. Maybe they'll push something to us."

As guides go, Ed was unusual in that he was straightforward and honest about the task at hand. Skilled and experienced as a big-game hunter, he remained realistic about the difficulties involved in locating and killing elk, particularly for hunters unaccustomed to the West.

There were, for example, horses to consider: Many hunters are unwilling or unable to ride them where they need to be ridden, including nearly straight up and/or straight down. And mountains: Many hunters are in poor physical condition, leaving them too immobile to have a reasonable chance at success. And marksmanship: Many hunters, particularly those native to the eastern United States, are too unfamiliar with their rifles to score on shots that Western guides think reasonable—specifically, anything under 300 yards, whether at level, 90-degree ascent, or 90-degree descent.

"They just haven't shot their guns enough under these conditions to know what their bullets will do," Ed said.

Take the ballistics of the .270. If the gun is zeroed at 200 yards, a standard 150-grain bullet will fall 3.8 inches at 250 yards, 9.7 inches at 300 yards, 29.2 inches at 400 yards, and 62.2 inches at 500 yards.

Some hunters and guides employ portable range finders to determine these distances, but often they are too bulky and too time-consuming to be effective. It is better if the hunter knows how to use the duplex hairs of this scope to judge distance, though this too is an inexact science.

The slope factor must also be considered. If the animal is 300 yards away, and the slope, either up or down, is 45 degrees, the hunter must multiply the distance by .70. The multiplier changes with the degree of slope: at 25 degrees, the figure is .91; at 35 degrees, .82. The result—210 yards—is the amount of horizontal range the hunter should consider when firing the rifle. If the rifle is zeroed at 200 yards, he can hold precisely on the animal and expect to connect. But if he fails to consider the slope and instead considers only the bullet drop—9.7 inches at 300 yards—he'll shoot high by that much.

"It's hard enough to find good bulls," Ed said. "Many times, it's even harder to hit them."

I was kneeling behind a spruce at 10,500 feet, snow blowing across the ridge in sheets. Improve conditions by 50 percent and it would still be a blizzard.

I had given up watching for elk, or for the hunters who were supposedly riding up the opposite ridge toward me, or for Ed, who had become restless and walked to the canyon below hoping to jump a bull. Wind and snow came so hard I could only cover my face and wait it out, the protection of the tree approximating that of a mobile home in a hurricane.

I thought of the transitions I had made during the last seven days. I had come to camp to kill an elk, and quickly. The thought of riding down the mountain, pack horse in tow, its panniers flush with the quarters of a freshly drawn bull was one I had entertained regularly, with a fascination bordering on fanaticism. So intent was I on consummating my efforts that I had given little thought to what usually provides pleasure on such outings—the actual process of hunting.

But by now I had become fatalistic about my chances for success. I had missed a shot at a bull, something I had not thought likely, and in

59

the time since had not seen any others. With increasing regularity I was broaching the possibility of not taking an elk.

Thus I had made a decision: Elk or no elk, I would leave the Rockies with something; if not a bull, then a better understanding of the animal and the skills required to hunt it. As I saw it, an education was available here and the tuition had already been paid.

My first lessons came on a day John and I hunted together.

We rode out of camp well before sunup and didn't return until nightfall. In the process we found mule deer and black bear. We also snuck to within 225 yards of a half-dozen elk, all cows and calves, lying on a snow-covered hillside.

Over lunch that day we talked about big-game hunts that have taken John from Africa to Alaska, where, among other species, he has hunted grizzly bear, polar bear, and sheep.

"A big-game hunter can do many things to improve his chances of succeeding," John said. "For one, he should be able to ride a horse and do it well enough so he can concentrate on his hunting, not on the horse itself. It's very important to be alert to surrounding country. Some hunters ride right by elk.

"Also, when a hunter sees an animal, it helps to be able to get off the horse quickly and get the gun out of the scabbard. Everything happens very fast in this kind of hunting. Opportunities for elk don't come along that often, and those who are able to see an elk, dismount, and put themselves in positions to shoot quickly have an advantage over other hunters.

"Other things are important, too, but the most important skill a big-game hunter needs is the ability to shoot well and shoot fast. Some shots are very, very difficult, and misses are understandable. But many shots that are missed are good shots that could have been made if the hunter knew his gun."

What necessitates refined hunting skills is the nature of elk, *Cervus canadensis*. They are animals of uncanny survival skills, with superb hearing, eyesight, and sense of smell. Moreover, elk possess a keen intelligence—what Ed refers to as a sixth sense.

"You watch them from a distance and you know they can't see you. But still, somehow, they sense that you're there and they move out of sight into heavy cover."

Steve and his hunters came over the ridge, and Ed returned from his push in the canyon below. Everyone had the same story: no elk. We broke for lunch, then split up again, with Ed and I beginning a circuitous and complicated journey back to camp, largely through uncharted territory.

Not long after the trip began I spotted a bull, at least a four-point (Western count), as it crossed a ridge 75 yards ahead of us. The animal appeared suddenly, rising from the canyon to the left, and disappeared just as suddenly into the canyon to the right.

It happened so quickly that the elk vanished before mental validation could be made. For a moment I wasn't sure I had seen what I thought I saw.

"Did you see that bull?"

Ed said, "No."

"I'm sure I saw it. Right ahead of us. It was a big animal."

We rode ahead quickly, the horses seeking solid footing as they high-stepped their way over the countless fallen trees that littered the ridge. Where I saw the animal cross we pulled up and dismounted. I yanked the .270 from its scabbard.

"Here are the tracks."

We inspected the evidence, then remounted, following, in a general way, the path the elk had taken. But the canyon bottom was 1,000 feet beneath us and thick with spruce. He could disappear anywhere. Our one hope was that he would present himself by some mistake or miscalculation, appearing momentarily, perhaps, on the opposite canyon wall.

Ed had hunted this canyon only twice before and as a result paths for the horses were nonexistent. The degree of descent was perhaps 55 percent, making it difficult for the animals to find solid footing as we side-sloped our way along the canyon wall, parallel to the bottom. Lucky periodically wheezed and snorted, reminders of his discontent.

A short while later Ed said: "To get back to camp, we're going to have to go to the bottom of this canyon and up the opposite side. It's pretty steep. We better lead them down."

We dismounted and, for a brief time, crawled and slid down the canyon wall, the horses following immediately behind, forelegs straight, rear haunches coiled. Traction was nearly impossible. On two occasions Lucky would have run over me had I not jumped to the side.

Finally, Ed said: "Grab your gun and turn Lucky loose. The horses will have to find their own way down."

I pulled the .270 from its scabbard and slapped Lucky on the butt. "Every man for himself," I said. "I'll follow you."

We made it down in short order, each employing variations of free-fall maneuvers previously unseen in these mountains. At the bottom we watered the horses in a small stream, then began our ascent.

It was about midway up the opposite canyon wall that I saw tan and brown, colors distinct to elk, through the trees. I jumped off Lucky, pulled the gun from its scabbard, and ran maybe 60 yards ahead of Ed, who tended the horses.

When I had a clear line of vision, I fell to one knee and jacked a shell into the chamber. Above me by 40 yards I could see three elk. One was a cow; the heads of the other two remained hidden by trees. I aligned the cross-hairs on the foreshoulder of one of the animals. As I did, it moved. Cow. I moved the gun to the third elk. As I did I could see that it, too, was a cow.

I returned to Ed and the horses.

I said, "I must not be living right."

The sun was gaining on the western horizon, and I knew the hunt would soon be ended. No one but myself and Ed and John would care whether or not I took an elk, but this perspective offered little comfort. In terms of preparation I had covered all the bases and the feeling of being owed a return on investment was unavoidable.

Ed reached the top of the ridge ahead of me and spotted four elk moving out of the canyon below and up the opposite side. The area was nearly devoid of trees and a shot, though long, would have been possible. But three of the animals were cows and the last a calf. We rode on.

Now I had given my thoughts over to fantasy. I thought about the Ute Indians who once rode their ponies on these lands and the elk that must have abounded then. I thought about hunts with the Indians and long shots by bow and arrow across meadows iridescent with sunlight. I thought about elk hides stretched and drying as hunters in tattered robes encircled a campfire, pipe passing from one to another. I thought about heavy snows and about Ute following elk to lower elevations, their heavily loaded travois dragging behind riderless horses. I thought of all this amid the gathering darkness and said to Lucky, "What the hell."

Then on the face of a wooded canyon maybe 800 yards distant I saw what appeared to be an elk. I reined in Lucky and whistled to Ed, who dismounted and glassed the canyon with binoculars. When he dropped the glasses, he nodded "yes" and indicated with his hand that I should tie my horse.

He whispered, "It's a bull."

We made our way by foot down the canyon and along a small ridge that ran between the horses and where the elk had stood. When I fell behind, Ed, more accustomed to the thin air, offered to carry my gun. "We don't have much time," he said.

When we reached an elevation equal to that of the elk we inched over the intermediate ridge. We saw nothing and crawled ahead still further, seeking refuge as we did behind oversized ponderosa pines.

Now we were maybe 200 yards from the spot where the elk had stood.

63

Ed saw the animal first.

"There's another one. And another. There's at least three, maybe four. Find a tree to brace your gun."

I wound the sling around my left arm and snugged the rifle forearm against a small spruce. Through the scope I could see the animals clearly, all cows except the one whose head remained hidden. We figured him to be our bull.

Ed said: "They're starting to move. Aim at the opening just ahead of them. When the bull appears there, shoot."

In single file the animals stepped out, moving left to right. One by one they walked through an opening maybe three-quarters the length of their bodies.

One cow. Two cow. Three cow.

I clicked off the safety and moved my right index finger inside the trigger guard. Next to me lay Ed, binoculars pressed against his face.

The animal eased into the opening.

Ed said: "Dammit!"

It was a cow. Either we had been mistaken in our initial appraisal—altogether possible considering the distance involved—or the bull we had seen had given us the slip.

Ed went for the horses. I remained where I was, continuing my vigil until he returned, when I unloaded the .270 and filed it in its scabbard.

Now it was dark and snow began to fall. I turned my collar against the cold and scratched Lucky behind his ears. I put my foot in the stirrup and climbed aboard. Camp would be better than an hour's ride away. Except for the sound of the horses' hooves the mountain night was silent.

Cowboy Cutting

Lucky isn't the only horse I've known. About 10 years back, I had spent a cool July evening watching ropers, bronc riders, and barrel racers compete in a two-bit rodeo in Livingston, Montana, the kind civic types schedule to appease local cowboys during community celebrations.

What I remember most about the evening was not the rodeo, but, later, the visage of a creaky old ranch hand walking into a small cafe, his flat-bed truck and stock trailer parked on the street, three or four horses inside the trailer, rocking the rig gently.

The man, his legs bowed, straw cowboy hat on his head, sat at the cafe counter, drank a cup of coffee and ate a sandwich, then walked out. Before he did, he pulled up a pant leg of his worn blue jeans, reached into his boot, and extracted a money clip, from which he peeled off a couple of bills, laying them on the counter.

I thought: This is Montana, and that's a cowboy.

Now I am in Montana again, this time in Big Timber with a horse of my own. I am about to amble into an arena to compete against 20 or so other riders in an event known as cutting, the point of which is to separate—cut—one or more cows from a herd and keep the two factions apart for 2½ minutes. Most of this is done with the horse on a loose rein.

For me, accomplishing a winning ride will be difficult, because some riders in my class could well be the sons and daughters of the cowboy I had seen a decade ago, horsemen and women who have ridden for years. This is not a thought that boosts my self-confidence.

Which in part explains why I am hoping not so much to win this cutting as to stave off embarrassment, a not altogether unreasonable tack I've applied to other life ventures, and one especially appropriate in this instance because I have ridden a horse seriously only since April. It was then that I purchased Doc Lynx Too, a nine-year-old, bald-faced dark bay gelding, the deal sealed over the phone, my money sent to a Tennessee horseman by bank transfer, the animal acquired sight unseen.

This dial-an-animal approach to horse buying is not without risk. Leg and foot problems, especially those attendant to cutting horses, can, in a heartbeat, sentence horses to lives lazing in pastures or, worse, to no lives at all. What's more, not every horse is a cutting horse, and not every cutting horse is a winner, a consideration that, if not properly weighed, can commit a cutter to a life of bad days, one after another.

Still, Lynx's former owner was confident the transaction would benefit everyone concerned, an assertion he supported with a guarantee. He also trotted out the fact that Lynx, a quarter horse, was "bred and born in Texas," adding that, "If you can ride him, he can win," words I understood to be both inspiration and warning.

It was a cold day in spring when Lynx was shipped by commercial horse van from Tennessee to a thoroughbred farm near Chicago. Pulling a borrowed trailer, I drove to Chicago to bring farther north still a horse I didn't even know how to saddle.

Small wonder that, en route home, with Lynx blanketed and following behind me, I felt the sense of disassociation common to people who have only the vaguest idea what they are doing.

Ahead of me in my class in Big Timber had ridden celebrity cowboys and real cowboys, the former including actor Michael Keaton of *Batman* and other movie fame.

Keaton owns a ranch up valley from Big Timber and is a relative

66

newcomer to the sport. Still, atop a pretty fancy horse, he marked a 73 on his ride, a fantasy-level score I had only imagined in my limited showings in Minnesota and South Dakota.

The best I had done so far on Lynx was a 70, and I had marked that only the day before. Unfortunately, 70 is considered an average ride in cutting, nothing more. Sixty is the equivalent of zero, and 80 is the highest score possible. But nobody gets an 80, not even here at the four-day Sweet Grass County Cutting, one of the biggest such events in the world.

Having strapped splint boots onto Lynx's legs and cinched the saddle tight, I sit momentarily atop Lynx outside the arena, my eyes fixed blankly on nothing in particular. My game plan, such as it is, comes down to this: If I can cut a couple of decent cows and maintain a deep saddle seat for a few minutes, I figure I have a chance of leaving the pen as inconspicuously as I plan to ride in.

In the absence of such good fortune, events could turn sour, or what one longtime cutter calls "go western," in which the performance skews toward the unpredictable, cows and horses running amok. Under these circumstances, people can get hurt.

I nudge a spur against Lynx's flank, popping him suddenly forward before stopping him just as quickly with a slight tightening of the reins. Then I back him a step, turn him hard, and roll him over his hocks. The quickness of his responses tells me he's ready.

The rider who has just finished his cutting comes out of the arena. There's no smile on his face as his name and hometown—somewhere in California—and his score, a 66, are given by the public-address announcer. In Sweet Grass County, a 66 won't earn you enough money to buy a beer.

Adjusting my cowboy hat (western clothing is required in cutting), I ride into the arena and await placement of the four riders who will be helping me. Two of them, called "herd holders," generally remain in the arena corners, one on each side of a herd of maybe 15 cows. Their job is to keep the herd from scattering while a cow is being cut. The other two riders are positioned to "turn back" cows that are cut, in essence forcing the animals back toward the cutter and the action.

Once my help is in position, I raise my right arm, signaling the timekeeper I am ready to enter the herd. Then I ease Lynx cautiously toward the far end of the pen, where our cows await.

For me, it's at this time that cutting assumes some of the qualities of an out-of-body experience. Part of me knows I am on a 1,000-pound animal and am about to turn him loose, giving him his head to do as he pleases. Another part of me, the out-of-body part, is somehow separate from the action and above the arena, hovering safely out of harm's way and reminding me continuously what Bob McCutcheon, my trainer from River Falls, Wisconsin, has taught me these past few months.

"Take your time. Relax.

"Push plenty of cows in front of you so you have plenty to cut from.

"Take your time. Relax.

"Set the cows up so that, ideally, you cut one in the middle of the pen.

"Take your time. Relax.

"When you have a cow cut and all other cows are behind you, drop your rein hand to the horse's neck.

"Take your time. Relax.

"Sit back on your pockets. Slump your back. Hold tightly with one hand on the saddle horn. Keep your heels down.

"Enjoy the ride."

The cows, Hereford crosses, I think, weighing 700 pounds, maybe more, part nervously as Lynx and I enter their ranks. Flanked by my herd holders, one on each side, I spur Lynx gently forward, pushing maybe a dozen head away from the back fence, toward the center of the arena.

Now comes the tricky part.

Over the summer, competing in a handful of Midwest cuttings, I've come to understand that a rider can't consistently mark good scores if he doesn't set up, or cut, a cow in the middle of the pen, meaning approximately equidistant from the left and right sides. A judge won't award points, or at least not very many points, to riders who "trap" cows against the arena sides.

Instead, points are given most often when horse and rider are quick enough to anticipate a cow's intended move, then jump quickly left or right, trapping the cow and forcing it in the opposite direction. The best horses do this with such athleticism and style that, as a bystander, you can, while watching, involuntarily suspend breathing, so awestruck are you at the sight of a horse splayed almost literally on its belly, popping left, popping right, quicker than the cow, quicker, even, than Magic Johnson.

The best riders, meanwhile, sit atop their horses in a manner that doesn't hinder their movement, the rider's legs and spurs the only tools with which he guides the action.

Lynx and I square off against a big white-faced cow positioned nearly in the center of the arena. Dropping my rein hand to Lynx's neck, I slump in the saddle, driving my heels toward the ground. Above me, I hear my voice and Bob McCutcheon's words: "Relax. Take your time."

When the cow realizes she has been separated from the herd, she bolts quickly right, trying to get around Lynx and me. Lynx counters with an even quicker move. Check. The cow jumps left. Lynx counters again. Checkmate.

Determined cows have been known to run over horses and riders, and the cow in front of Lynx and me pauses briefly to weigh, I think, just how determined she is planning to be. Lynx, his legs already somewhat akimbo, gives the cow still more to consider when he crawls even lower, coiling himself downward, quivering in anticipation of the cow's next move.

Then, as suddenly as the cow stopped, she starts again, scrambling right, left, then right, sometimes being trapped by Lynx in the middle of the pen, other times running "wall to wall." Sitting low, I push back on the saddle horn to hold myself in place when Lynx locks down and turns with the cow.

After about 40 seconds, the cow turns away and I quit her, meaning I lift the reins with my left hand and place my right hand on Lynx's neck, indicating the cow now can be allowed to return to the herd.

Estimating I have a least a minute, maybe a minute and a half, remaining in my ride, I turn Lynx quietly over his hocks and ride back into the herd.

In north Texas last winter, leaning against a cold steel cow pen, I watched my first competitive cutting. What struck me about the event, in addition to the horse work, was the seemingly disproportionate number of good riders with names like "Travis," "Clint," "Buck," and "Joe."

I thought: I have the wrong name for this sport. And I come from the wrong state.

Texas, that's where cowboys live. Oklahoma, too. And Montana. Not Minnesota. Not Wisconsin—except perhaps for the odd ranch hand incarcerated here, maybe on a federal rap.

The point is, I'm deficient on the dust quotient. I have the boots, the spurs, the hat and shirt. I even have a pickup truck, albeit one too clean and dentless for serious ranch work. But I don't have the twang, and I'm not yet fully convincing at cutting-horse rap, practice as I do the expressions, "He can go wall to wall. But he ain't no marker. Got no stop. No pop. No trap."

That said, on this day, Lynx has all of that and more. My second cow, even livelier than the first, allows Lynx to trap him in the middle of the pen. Things go well, so well that even I, inexperienced as I am, can sense a pretty good run building.

The buzzer sounds as Lynx stops hard and sends my hat flying. I quit the cow and dismount, stepping down for my now dirty hat.

As I do, the public-address announcer says, "That was Dennis Anderson on Doc Lynx Too, with a score of 71½."

A long pause follows, then, "Dennis Anderson is from . . . Houston, Texas."

Houston! Texas!

Yes!

"Correction. That's Houlton, Wisconsin."

I dust off my hat, climb into the saddle, and ride Lynx from the pen, happy enough that our score has earned Lynx and me a fifth-place tie, paying money I plan to keep in the safest place I know.

My boot.

Retrieving
the British Way

Eight-thirty in the morning and the corner of a muddy stubble field near Gorebridge, Scotland, is filling with cars.

Peugeot. Mercedes. Ford. Windshield wipers flapping, the vehicles follow one another onto the field, brake lights beaming as drivers slow to avoid yellow Labradors, black Labradors, golden retrievers. In the distance, a handsome flat-coated retriever, head held high, observes with feigned detachment.

From one vehicle steps John Halstead and his wife, Sandra, who have with them three dogs: Mark, Dean, and the injured Breeze (the reigning British retriever champion), all black Labradors, all Field Trial Champions, all bearing the banner of Drakeshead, the Halstead's kennel name.

From another vehicle emerge Suzan Scales and her Labrador Manymills Milady. From yet another vehicle comes professional trainer Richard Webb. With him is the four-year-old female black Labrador Birdbrook Jet. The dog belongs to Lady Allerton.

Her Majesty Queen Elizabeth II is not attending Great Britain's Retriever Championship this year. A dog handler and retriever field-trial judge in her own right, she has not qualified a dog for the event.

That fact has not precluded her attendance in other years. When the retriever finals were held on the Duke of Wellington's estate in 1984, the Queen attended, suffering, as did others, the day-long rains that so often frequent the British Isles in December, her head covered only by a silk scarf.

But that was two years ago. On this overcast day in Scotland, 31 dogs are competing for the Retriever Championship of Great Britain, an event unique in the world of sporting animals, and one that is gaining increasing attention among United States retriever breeders, trainers, and field-trialers.

In recent decades, indiscriminate breeding has fed a vastly increased demand for retrievers in the United States (more than 150,000 retrievers were registered with the American Kennel Club in 1985). The result has been dilution of the breeds' working abilities (relatively few retrievers are actually hunted or trialed) and increased incidences of hip dysplasia, central progressive retinal atrophy, retinal dysplasia, and other physical maladies.

"The possible consequence of what is happening to U.S. retrievers is genetic disaster," warns the noted American gundog writer Richard Wolters. "Every sporting dog that has become popular with the general public in the United States has fallen in decline. The Irish setter is a good example. The same is happening to American retrievers."

What is more, to win American field trials today, one must campaign a retriever that is smart, trainable, strong, durable, fast, and possessed of a mettle that will allow it to withstand a grueling training regimen. Often this includes use of the electric collar, a training aid that is humane and effective if properly employed, but one that the British abjure, claiming it unnecessary with their type of retriever, which they suggest is "softer," easier to train, and more willing to please than its American counterpart.

Many U.S. hunters and other lay retriever trainers would perhaps agree on this latter point. It is from American field-trial stock that they purchase their gundogs—they have few other sources—and it is from this gene pool that many a frustration has been born. Too often in recent years, puppies of American field-trial retrievers have grown to adult-

73

hood hyperactive, bull-headed, or in some instances just plain too "hot" for the non-professional to train, or even contain.

Thus, many observers believe a two-headed monster has emerged among American retrievers, one the progeny of indiscriminate breeding, the other, ironically, the progeny of breeding that is too discriminate. "Diseased nature often times breaks forth in strange eruptions," Shakespeare once wrote.

Perchance he spoke of retrievers?

What you notice first about British retriever trials is the silence. Handlers speak to one another in hushed tones, as they do when they address their dogs. Even their whistles are quieter than those favored by Americans.

You notice next the dress of the trial's participants and gallery. Many of the men wear silk ties or ascots with tattersall shirts. Wool caps, shooting coats, walking sticks, and knee-length rubber boots—"wellies"—are standard attire.

The women are no less smartly attired, and nearly everyone, man and woman alike, wears dark green or brown Barbour rainwear, or its equivalent.

In part, this is the British style. These are a reserved people, proper in their mannerisms and not given to excess, either in voice or dress.

"But the real point, of course, is not to frighten the game, either by action or by the wearing of brightly colored clothing," said Major Morty Turner-Cooke.

A retired Army officer and former professional retriever trainer, Turner-Cooke is attending the trial as an observer and reporter for a British gundog magazine, having narrowly failed to qualify his black Labrador for the championship.

"Not frightening the game" is important in Britain because, unlike American retriever trials, British trials are held on actual hunts, or "shoots" as they're called. Such shoots are conducted on private estates, and the retriever club sponsoring a field trial is the invited guest of the estate owner.

On this day, the International Gundog League, organizer of the championship, is the guest of the banker P. H. J. de Vink, on whose 12,000-acre Arniston Estate the trial is being held.

Simultaneously, de Vink and his guests—some of whom have flown in from the Continent and all of whom are shooting the fine double guns of Europe, among them Holland and Hollands and Purdeys—will conduct a shoot while the retriever club and its entrants conduct a trial.

In part, this arrangement explains why typical British field trials are limited to 24 participants, selected by lot from the 100 or more that might apply for entry.

"There is neither the room nor the time to evaluate more than a limited number of dogs during a two-day shoot," said Turner-Cooke.

At least half of a typical trial will be conducted during "walk-ups," the term given to a line of hunters proceeding through a field shooting game (pheasant mostly, but also rabbit, hare, and gray partridge) as it arises.

Six or seven dogs and their handlers will typically be "in line" with the shooters—"guns" the British call them—as they walk the field.

Also in line will be various field-trial judges and stewards, as well as two or three game carriers and perhaps that many or more "beaters," whose job it is to help flush game.

British field-trial retrievers are never used for putting game to wing. They are instead kept at heel during the walk-up, their handlers instructed not to address them in any fashion. Should a dog stray from heel or break from line when a shot is fired, he and his handler are dismissed from the trial.

"This is just good manners," said Turner-Cooke. "But you must understand as well that most pheasants shot on estates in England have been raised, released, and tended throughout the summer and into the shooting season at considerable expense to the landlord. In U.S. cur-

75

rency, a pheasant put before the gun during a walk-up has a value of about $15. And pheasants put before the gun during a driven shoot, wherein many beaters are employed to push the birds over a line of guns, are valued at about $22 apiece.

"Consequently, it is absolutely required that our retrievers be steady to the gun. Otherwise, during a walk-up, the game will be frightened out of gun range, and the shoot ruined. Worse, during a driven shoot, a dog that breaks or squeaks [whines] may frighten the birds back over the beaters, again ruining the shoot. That's why a dog in a trial is never allowed to issue the slightest noise, or it will be disqualified."

During a walk-up, anything flushed within range of the line is shot—or shot at—and the dogs must retrieve whatever falls, be it of wing or fur. When game is downed, the judges decide which dog will be sent and notify its handler. Sometimes game is shot by a gun to the right of the line, but a dog to the far left is selected for the retrieve.

"This is another difference between our trials and yours," Turner-Cooke said. "You try to make each retrieve uniform for each dog during a trial. We take them as they come. Some of our dogs will get more difficult retrieves than others. The judges take this into account in their evaluations."

If a dog is unable to find a downed bird (some cripples may run 100 yards before a dog is sent), another dog is selected. If the second dog also fails, the judges may, if they believe the bird recoverable, send a third dog.

If the third dog finds the bird, the first two are eliminated. This is called "wiping the eye" of the first two dogs.

But if the third dog fails to find the bird, the judges likely will inspect the area themselves. If they also fail to "pick" the bird, the second and third dog may be allowed to remain in the trial. But because the first dog failed to capitalize on the advantage of fresh scent, it probably will be dropped.

"Our retrievers are encouraged to hunt the bird," Turner-Cooke said. "They must mark where a bird falls, and do it exactly, so they can go quickly to the fall. Once there, they must hunt hard. In most instances, we do not offer them a lot of direction. The dog is instead judged on its hunting ability. This may entail trailing a bird for hundreds of yards, even jumping fences. But the dog must know how to track the fallen bird and discard other birds that come in its path."

On the afternoon of the first day, Roy Burns was asked to send his four-year-old female golden retriever for a pheasant that initially fell only 15 yards distant. But by the time the judge allowed the dog to be sent, the bird had run a hundred yards ahead through the thick underbrush of the turnip field being hunted.

At first Burns allowed the dog to hunt the area of the fall. Then he ordered her to "get out" in an attempt to put the animal in pursuit of the fast-disappearing pheasant. The dog hesitated then took the scent and pushed ahead 100 yards, before shifting to the right 75 yards. Then the dog moved ahead still another 125 yards and disappeared over a hill.

The dog had followed the bird's trail exactly. In the process, she had incidentally flushed other pheasants. But she disregarded these birds completely, even though some were felled by the guns.

Minutes later the dog again appeared atop the hill, a colorful rooster in her mouth.

"Well done," a judge whispered as the dog returned.

By the afternoon of the second day, eight dogs remained in contention. Three were golden retrievers, two were yellow Labradors, and three were black Labradors.

In their final test, the eight were positioned on a narrow strip of land between a lake and a stand of woods. This was a driven shoot in which pheasants would be pushed out of the woods, over the guns, and with luck the guns would drop the birds into the lake.

The dogs would be tested for steadiness during the shoot and, later, for ability to retrieve in water. Controlled chaos erupted as the beaters, who were flushing the birds, neared the guns.

The beaters whistled. As birds took wing, the beaters yelled, "Ov-ah! Ov-ah!" signaling that a bird was about to appear ov-ah head.

When the shooting began, birds dropped all around the dogs. One even fell on a dog.

But the dogs remained steadfast on their haunches.

The water retrieves that followed were simple compared to water retrieves in U.S. trials. Because Great Britain has relatively few lakes, gundog enthusiasts there place little emphasis on water work.

At day's end, the fast and stylish five-year-old Field Trial Champion Breeze of Drakeshead had successfully defended his title, and was again named the best retriever in Great Britain.

The webbing cut between two toes, Breeze had competed with a bandaged rear foot.

Are British retrievers better than American retrievers?

Doubtless, British dogs could not win American retriever trials. American trials are too exacting. A 250-yard "blind" retrieve, for instance, is not uncommon in our trials, yet is unheard of in Britain.

Conversely, rare would be the American dog that could win a British field trial (even if Britain's six-month quarantine restriction on incoming dogs didn't effectively prevent American dogs from competing, and vice versa). Many U.S. field-trial dogs are too unsteady, too noisy, and too mechanical to win in Britain.

Field trials aside, which dogs would be better champions in the field?

Forget it.

I have friends on both sides of the Atlantic.

Canine and otherwise.

Boogie

Some years ago, near the end of October, my yellow Lab, Boogie, and I were in a frozen slough near Chokio, in west-central Minnesota. The idea was to put up a pheasant or two but the birds weren't cooperating, hens flushing now and again at our feet and in the near distance, but the warier roosters rising only occasionally and then at the nether reaches of shotgun range.

The dog and I hunted all afternoon and had nothing to show for it. Complicating events was the fact that Boogie was dying, which I knew and he probably did, too. But birds or not you can't hunt in the dark. So when dusk approached we headed back to the truck, walking as we did a final piece of cover that held some promise.

About halfway down the line Boogie showed heightened interest and soon a big rooster cackled up. It had begun to snow, and to shoot the bird I had to squint into a brisk wind, firing twice and felling the pheasant with the second shot. Boogie made the retrieve but shortly thereafter tipped over, suffering yet another seizure, his four legs stiffening, tongue limp to one side, as he convulsed beneath what was by now a heavy snowfall.

Jacking the last shell from the chamber, I leaned my gun against a clump of stiff cattails and summed up our little entourage: A dead pheasant. A sick dog. And me.

When I knew it had to be done, that there could be no more delay, I called my vet and we talked. We talked and when he concurred I said, "How about five o'clock tomorrow?" Few people would be in the office then. "Fine," he said, though it was his afternoon off.

The night I called the vet, Boogie was treated more regally than usual. This took some doing. I find no shame in admitting I routinely treat my dogs as I do people. In some instances, I treat dogs better.

So Boogie, now eight years old, got his usual attention and then some. His food treats and rawhide bones were more plentiful than is customary, his walk longer, and his pats on the head more prolonged. And just as the lights went out, he got the one offer he could never refuse: an invitation to hop atop the bed.

Such an opportunity was usually limited to Sunday mornings, when in our house fat newspapers are read slowly over dark coffee. On this day, one or more dogs are invited to join in the merriment, their crumpling of newsprint and shedding of hair the only drawbacks, and minor ones at that.

Sunday morning aside, it had been a long time since Boogie's inquiring eyes had met with an approving nod and a pat on the mattress, a surefire invitation to jump onto what he viewed as queen-sized heaven. The offer surprised him, but he wasted little time. He coiled tightly his nearly 90-pound body, then gracefully sprang aloft and onto the bed.

As was his style, he landed as if already asleep, seeming to say, "It's too late to change your mind, boss. I'm here, and I won't be awake for a long time."

He had perfected this trick over the years, especially on hunting trips, when on occasion we would stay in motels. He knew he was part of the gang when we hunted, and he knew too that the hunt would not be the same without him. Just as he would not hunt without me, I would not hunt without him, which is why he graced more than one motel bed in his day.

The next morning there was Christmas shopping to be completed,

80

and my wife and I allowed Boogie, the eldest of our three dogs, to come along. This, too, was an unexpected treat. But he took it in stride, sitting in the back seat, damp nose pressed against frosted windows, tail wagging at passing cars.

As always, he wore his smile—a grin, really—that, to my mind, was unique. Most of it was his nature, but part of it, I think, was due to his excessive medication. He was, you see, severely epileptic.

But that was not his real problem. Thanks to the medication, he lived with the epilepsy, and quite nicely.

His real problem, it seemed, began almost two years earlier when he suffered from what University of Minnesota veterinarians diagnosed as a brain tumor. A spinal tap and brain scan failed to yield definitive results, so the diagnosis was never confirmed. But confirmation or not, he could not stand without wobbling and falling.

While he was hospitalized at the university, I visited him nearly every day, walking him in fields, picking him up as he fell, righting him once, twice, three times, then watching helplessly as he fell again.

Through it all, he only grinned.

For whatever reason, Boogie defied the odds. Doctors said the tumor would likely return and he would die within a few months, but it didn't and he didn't. Instead, he continued to hunt. Quebec, Ontario, Manitoba, the Dakotas, Minnesota, and Iowa. Two more seasons, he continued to hunt.

But he never really recovered. His only physical deficiency was a slight head-tilt. But there was more to it than that. He was newly distant and less enthusiastically obedient.

He was, in a word, detached.

Then, in his last days, the days before I called the vet, he appeared uncomfortable. Rather than lying on the floor, relaxing, he spent his time sitting at my side, head on my knee, eyes fixed to mine.

I tried to interpret what he was saying. I figured he was telling me it was over. He knew it, and he wanted me to know it.

81

So I called the vet, let Boogie spend a night on the bed, took him shopping, and just before we went to the vet's office, hunted with him a last time.

We didn't get anything on our final hunt. Boogie worked hard, hunted close, and checked in intermittently for affectionate pats on the head. But there were no birds, and finally I sat next to a tree, wool pants against the snow, and said: "What the hell. We've had our share."

At four o'clock we headed to the vet's office. On the way, I let Boogie sit up front, mainly because he deserved it, but also because a little dog hair on a pickup's front seat only adds to its character. Or at least that's the way I figure it.

And Boogie was some character. He was not the best hunting dog that has graced this earth. But neither am I the best hunter. Which is why I forgave him his weaknesses, just as he seemingly forgave my missed shots, misguided orders, and poorly placed decoys.

En route to our destination, we made a brief stop at a hamburger joint, where I bought Boogie an ice-cream sundae, his favorite treat. Then we went directly to the vet's office, parked in a dark lot, and walked into an empty lobby.

The vet, Wayne Scanlon of White Bear Animal Hospital, had treated Boogie for years. Wayne asked me if I still wanted to be with Boogie at the end. I said I did. It was only right.

So we walked into a room and I held Boogie. The needle went into his leg and soon he was dead, his body limp on the floor.

His pain was gone at last.

Mine had just begun.

Smelting

It is a warm and windless afternoon along Minnesota's North Shore, and up and down its rocky coastline people are taking advantage of the blessings of springtime. At the extreme north, not far from the Canadian border, two men who should be working are instead fishing steelhead in the Flute Reed River. Farther south, near Lutsen, the garden-club women of Tofte, Schroeder, and Grand Marais are meeting over blueberry muffins and ice cream. And down the coast farther still, at the mouth of the Stewart River, three long-hairs are playing Mick Jagger tapes, drinking beer from dented cans of Miller High Life, passing around a tattered copy of *Playboy*, and waiting for the smelt to run.

They are not alone. Forty or so other men are also waiting. Some are sober; others are not. But those whose minds are clear enough to care are confused and somewhat dismayed that, despite exaggerations to the contrary, the smelt have been scarce this spring. In fact, for all practical purposes, there have been no smelt runs, at least not here, not at the Stewart.

Because of this, complaints are rife. It is not acceptable to some that the tiny fish that have run up this river in years past are not here this year. For them there is no such thing as an off year, no such thing as a year when the smelt just don't run up the Stewart.

"I'm not going smelting no more," said one salt-of-the-earth type, an old man whose waders are patched and double-patched. "I'm going to the FBI about this. I'll take care of this myself. I cleaned up Wisconsin, you know. Did it by myself, too. They were killing deer and selling them over there, and I followed them sumbitches for three days. I caught 'em and I turned 'em in, too.

"I don't think there are no smelt left to run," the old man said. "Them damn commercial fishermen are taking them all. They'll take more in one night than you can take in 10 years. I heard the state's going to sue them for 15 million dollars. *Fifteen million dollars.* 'Course I don't know if it's true. Some kid told me that."

These comments draw guffaws from some and agreement from others. "Damn right," one old man says. "You tell 'em," says another between tokes on a joint. "You tell 'em."

But most of these men are not interested in contacting the FBI or anyone else about smelt or the lack thereof. Instead, their intent is to have a good time, to relax and soak up the sunshine that shimmers on the lake and beats down on their pickups and campers.

"Tonight's the night," says one man in his twenties, his hand wrapped firmly around a can of Blatz. "They'll run tonight for sure. With this warm weather like this, I'm sure they'll run tonight."

One needn't be overly perceptive to realize this man is not participating in a Blatz taste test; at this point in his life, it is unlikely he could tell beer from Everclear. In fact, it would be safer to suggest he was testing his ability to endure the wicked spirits, not test them.

"We've been up here a week now," he says. "We're from the Cities and we're staying until they run. We don't care how long it takes, either, we're staying."

"That's a long time to be up here," one observer notes. "How do you pass the day?"

"We drink," he says. "We got nothin' better to do. I'm on unemployment, he's on social security, and the other two guys are retired. We're gonna stay until they run."

Stay until they run. That is what they intend to do, and in all probability it is what they will do. And not only at the Stewart. From the Lester near Duluth to the Poplar near Grand Marais, the men are gathered to wait for the smelt, to wait for the night when they can dip their wire nets into the river and pull them out flush and heavy with the squirming little fish. "They're running! The smelt are running!" These cries will echo up and down the coast. And they will not stop until the fish do.

But until then there are afternoons such as these, afternoons where hours are measured by the circles sea gulls make at the mouth of the river, or by oarboats that pass on the horizon. It is a lazy, sometimes depressing and sometimes invigorating way to pass the day. But, like the two guys on the Flute Reed playing hooky from work and the garden-club members meeting over lunch, it is part of springtime on the North Shore.

"I've been up here 25 years," said the old man who had single-handedly wiped out vice and corruption in Wisconsin. "'55, '65, '75, '80—yep, I've been here 25 years. Smelters have been here ever since then.

"But I ain't never seen a time like this when they didn't run. Never."

Bones

Come to the Exumas to bonefish and, like the smelters on the North Shore, at night you drink. Except that in the Exumas you drink to offset the parching effects of the sun. Then you walk from the place you are staying, skirting the harbor, and into George Town. Sam's. Two Turtles. Peace and Plenty. From these restaurants you pick one.

The old duck hunters and I had eaten at Two Turtles, the two of them opting for lobster, I the turtle, all of it broiled. Then we walked across the street and down a block to Peace and Plenty, where as usual old Lermon the bartender was holed up in a small room with low ceilings, a former slaves' quarters. Beneath a spinning overhead fan, the warm tropic air in constant motion, Lermon mixed one of his specialties, the Goombay Smash.

We took a seat, ordered drinks. At a table across from us were two U.S. Customs agents. I knew this because I had seen them earlier in the day through a marginally serious telescopic lens. At the time they were astern in a 61-foot-long Hatteras, tethered to which was a 40-foot muscle boat, powered almost unbelievably by four 200-horsepower Mercury outboards. Both boats belonged to Customs, confiscated earlier from drug runners, now working for the other side.

"You boys fishing?" I ask.

"You might say we're trolling," the one says.

The Bahamas have long been a favorite drop point for pilots flying from Colombia with cocaine and marijuana. They unload the stuff on small islands, where it is picked up by Florida-bound Bahamians, people who themselves have fast boats, not uncommonly powered by three Johnson 225-horsepower outboards. Looking at such machinery I think: enough to put a small ship up on a plane.

The boats and motors, together with U.S. Army Black Hawk helicopters stationed on the island and an outsized, jetliner-shaped radar balloon the U.S. Drug Enforcement Agency flies high over Great Exuma (tethered to the ground by cables), combine to galvanize for visiting bonefishermen an island milieu of secret agents, bootleggers, fish, rum, sailboats, conch chowder, sun, and mellowness, all of it presented in a kind of weird stage play suggestive of a "Miami Vice" episode gone awry.

The show would be played out in slow motion, cadence of the Caribbean.

Chasing bonefish is like chasing ghosts, and oftentimes as productive. But properly accomplished it is angling raised to art, the bonefisherman (assuming his success) himself becoming an artist.

Here's how to fish bones.

Get yourself a tide table showing times of incoming and outgoing tides. Ideally you want to fish the last two hours of the outgoing and the first two of the incoming. So if absolute low tide is at 9:00 A.M., you fish from 7:00 A.M to 11:00 A.M.

Unless, that is, you fish with Dick Hanousek of St. Paul, one of the old duck hunters whose addiction to bonefishing requires not hours-long vigils on the "flats" where bonefish can be found, but, rather, day-long outings so protracted that, were you not completely covered with clothing and sun block, you would fry like bacon in a truck stop, sizzled crisp.

"Isn't this great? This is great!" Hanousek will say.

And it is. But oftentimes for long periods you strain your eyes through Polaroid sunglasses, peering into clear, shin-deep water, looking for shadows, reflections, anything indicating the presence of one of the ocean's most mysterious finned creatures; a fish that, with the receding tide every six hours, swims from deep water to shallow in search of snails, crustaceans, and other food.

The idea when a bonefish is spotted is to lock and load in a hurry, to put your 10-foot fly rod in quick motion, laying line out, shooting, stretching the line a bit farther, then shooting it ahead a final time, hoping your tiny fly will fall unnoticed at a point not far in front of the fish.

You do this properly and you may entice the bonefish—which typically weigh between two and six pounds—to take the fly, provided you have stripped the line toward you in tantalizing fashion, darting the fly across the sandy bottom.

If a hook-up is made, the experience for the angler is roughly akin to that of hanging onto the stern of the U.S. Customs boat, the one with the four Merc 200s, and yelling, "Hit it!"

The translucent aquamarine-colored waters surrounding the Exumas, a string of more than 300 Bahamian islands and cays beginning about 30 miles below Nassau, are favorites not only with bonefishermen, tourists, and drug runners, but also with sailors—the wealthy, the not so wealthy, the down and out.

Each year, some 300 boats, mostly sail, anchor in the George Town harbor or a short distance away, off Stocking Island. The boats hail from nearly every port, Florida to New York, Minnesota to Louisiana. Some carry retirees, some the idle rich, some the vagabonds of the world, people who exist outside the margins of just about everything.

"I told my wife that when I die, just push me off the bow," says Hugh Simpson of Toronto, who with his wife Sue owns *She*, a 44-foot-long Roberts anchored just outside George Town. *She* has a destination of Venezuela generally, nowhere specifically.

Says Hugh: "All cruisers go through periods when you rethink the whole thing, when you wonder if what you're doing is right. Last month was particularly bad for us. We ran aground very seriously, and for 12 hours or so, the boat lay over on her side. Then, two days later, while leaving an anchorage where there were a number of other boats, our transmission got stuck in reverse and I couldn't stop the boat. We went through the entire anchorage backwards, almost hitting a couple of other boats, and almost running aground again.

"After that, we thought maybe we should take a break, maybe go home and stay with relatives for a while," Sue says. "But we decided instead to come down to George Town and see how it goes."

The old duck hunters and I have been on the flats five hours, one of them ahead of me and to my left 400 yards, the other to my right and behind. The day is hot, the sun merciless, the wind pushing 25 knots. Proper casting is tricky.

I have stopped wading. The water is barely more than ankle deep and I am doing a slow 360-degree spin, right hand holding my fly rod, maybe 30 feet of line stretched out at my feet. My intent when a fish is spotted is to get the line in the air and make the cast.

Meantime, I am daydreaming, thinking about food. The night before I had bought a half-dozen fresh conch off a fishing boat in the harbor. I had to vie with a handful of locals at the dock, young men who cut the conch from their shells and ate them fresh, still alive, still fibrillating, beating like a man's heart, and about the same size.

But what I had in mind was conch salad and cracked conch. I wanted to prepare it myself, having eaten too often recently in restaurants. So while waiting for the old duck hunters to return from errands in town, I sliced each conch, halving their thicknesses, then beat each of the pieces with a mallet, "bruising" them, as the locals say. Four pieces were diced for the salad, another six set aside for frying. And two I took to Nancy Bottomly, the woman who owns the apartment where we were staying.

Bottomly, who came to George Town from San Francisco in 1963, says about living in the Bahamas: "You can lead a simple life here. You don't need fancy cars or houses. And you're able to enjoy people. You do away with all the artifacts of the States. It's almost like a nudist colony. You are what you are what you are. You can't come down here and say I was a big deal in the States. Bahamians are good at reading people, and they wouldn't accept that."

Still spinning in the sand, watching the rush of the outgoing tide, I spot a bonefish 30 feet away. As the fish angles left, continuing its approach, I drop to one knee to minimize the chance the fish will see me. Then I false cast once and make my play.

The cast hits the mark, but the strong wind blows excess line behind me, wrapping it around a knife case threaded through the belt of my small fanny pack.

Turning to free the line, I feel the fish pick up the fly. But my inattentiveness prevents a connection.

The opportunity is lost.

Last day.

We've parked our beat-up rental car on an abandoned dirt road, walked through 300 yards of thick foliage and stepped onto the flats, miles and miles of sand covered by two feet of clear water.

We are trying to catch a fish to photograph with an underwater camera. The old duck hunters have fanned out, looking for bones, making intermittent casts to occasionally appearing fish. No luck.

Then, on the flat horizon, Dick, our most proficient angler, goes to his knees. He makes one cast, a second, then jumps upright, holding his rod high above him, right hand cupped beneath the reel as his line straightens, a bonefish taking his fly seaward with a velocity reminiscent of a carrier rocket-launching an F-18—fast, low, and hard.

Dick chases, stumbles once, tries to gain back enough line to control the fish. I move toward Dick, as does the other old duck hunter, who takes Dick's rod while Dick holds his camera under water and begins clicking.

Unnoticed by us a barracuda appears from behind, making a pass at the bonefish but missing its mark on the initial swing.

The 'cuda turns, accelerates, tries again.

This time its aim is truer, and the 'cuda smacks the bonefish enthusiastically, scissoring it almost exactly in half, leaving only a bloody stump dangling from the end of Dick's line.

"The blood will bring sharks," Dick says.

Within a few minutes sharks in fact come, two of them, small as these fish go, dorsal fins nonetheless protruding from the shallow water. Reasoning the tide has been pretty well fished out anyway, we angle toward shore, footsteps leaving slight swirls of sand in the water behind.

If the DEA's radar balloon suspended above Great Exuma is as good as the locals think, it might have tracked us moving through the water, through 300 yards of heavy foliage to our beat-up rental car and back to George Town, where we showered beneath cool water, washing away the day's sun and salt.

The balloon might even have seen us walk to town, skirting the harbor and settling in at Peace and Plenty, the old duck hunters and I ordering grouper in the restaurant before shuffling next door to the bar, where Lermon was mixing his specialty, the Goombay Smash, and where, just outside, a Bahamian band played a Harry Belafonte song about island living.

Palm trees swayed in the warm evening breeze. Bonefish had returned to deep water with the rising tide. Hugh and Sue Simpson were preparing to sail the next day toward Venezuela.

And somewhere on the dark water beyond, a U.S. Customs agent was strapping on a pair of night-vision glasses and throttling up four Merc 200s, preparing to do a little trolling of his own.

Big Water Bluebills

This morning, bluebills skittered overhead as we ran in the boats from where we camped to where we are hunting, the shoreline vaguely alight with florid aspens rustling in keening wind.

Now we are keeping a small warming fire burning and watching a string of two dozen decoys rock stupidly 30 yards out front.

The hope is the decoys will attract their feathered brethren and we will get some shooting.

Not much luck so far. Six hours, three cups of coffee, a too-dry sandwich, and a cheap cigar after arrival on this hard rock point and we, Willy and me, have in our possession two bills, a hen and a drake, both nicely plumed.

Sunset is three hours distant.

"Willy boy, the good news is that, should we become stranded on this island, we have enough ammunition to fire warning shots nonstop from now until December, maybe January," I said. "The bad news is we run out of toilet paper in a day, maybe two."

"Right."

Willy is listening, sort of, but mostly his stare is fixed on the horizon—left, right, center—eyes watching for ducks that, as anyone who has hunted bluebills knows, can appear from what seems like thin air.

On Lake of the Woods in Ontario, it happens like this.

You rise at 5:00 or 5:30 A.M., depending where on the 1,700-square-

mile lake you are camped. In our case, we are at a small resort just outside Morson, on the southwest end of the lake. And because we will
sometimes run 30 miles or more in boats to hunt, an early wake-up call
is to our advantage.

This is not an endorsement of such long trips. As the saying goes:
Don't attempt these maneuvers yourself. Lake of the Woods is big and
potentially treacherous, capable, in a brisk wind, of wave action that
would give pause to surfers.

After rising, there is breakfast, sandwich-making, the feeding of
dogs, and the filling of thermoses. The boat has been readied the night
before and its gas tanks filled, so when food and equipment are packed
in the predawn darkness and carted from cabin to dock, departure can
be made quickly, the lake and shoreline silhouetted to the east by the
light of the coming day.

Hunters who guide themselves on Lake of the Woods sometimes
do so alone but usually go out with friends. The problem with operating
without a professional guide—even my brother, Dick, who knows the
lake well, concedes—is that the potential exists (in a heartbeat) to hit a
rock pile or shallow reef and to take the lower unit off the outboard
motor, an accident that usually is the result of bad luck, poor judgment,
or both.

Whatever the circumstances, the appearance of an oil slick astern
is telltale of big-time misfortune.

Rock and boat collisions can also produce hull gashes and even
the rather grim possibility of death by cold water, far from, as the poet
Robert Service would say, "kith and kin."

"I like to see ducks fly and I like to shoot a few ducks," Dick had
said the day before, when he and a friend, Kevin Maki of Duluth, hunted
with Willy and me. Dick, who lives outside Eveleth, Minnesota, added:
"Lake of the Woods has elements that make duck hunting interesting
and adventurous. Big water. Big boats. Long runs. And bluebills."

Thinking about this, I toss another stick on the fire and light a second cigar, this one cheaper than the first. The dogs (we have three with us) are, with the exception of Chuck, the youngest, lying down and about to catch an afternoon nap. They had figured we'd be here for the day, and with few birds flying and even fewer to retrieve, the outing is growing longer and longer.

Looking at Willy, I see he, too, is nodding off, oblivious to the 30-knot wind kicking out of the north, decoys bobbing in a heavy chop of cold water.

Oblivious, too, to the flock of 15 or so bluebills that materialize without notice as if from a wave or cloud, flying just outside our decoys, moving quickly, right to left.

"Brrrrr, brrrrr."

The call awakened Willy and brought the dogs to their haunches.

Willy looked at me as though to determine if I was playing games with him, jolting him from sleep under the false pretense that there was reason to be awake. But he could tell by the expression on my face and the fact that I was hunched forward, keeping my head low, that there were birds in the area.

I pointed to the left, where the ducks, flying away from us now but still in tight formation, were rising very slightly and beginning a soft bank to the right.

I called again, "Brrrrr, brrrrr," hoping to entice the birds to complete their turn and vector back toward the decoys.

Willy whispered, "I think they'll make it."

He meant that with luck and if we hold tight the ducks might swing back, perhaps passing closer this time, within shooting range.

"Mark," I said, alerting the dogs to lift their heads and watch the sky for incoming birds.

In these circumstances, time freezes, the pitch and play of approaching ducks being mesmerizing, if not hallucinogenic. This is particularly true of bluebills, a species of diving duck that, unlike mallards and other puddle ducks, is capable of both reckless flight and dangerous living—traits that draw these hard-charging birds to decoys in every conceivable flight form save maybe inverted.

I finger the safety on my gun, ensuring myself of its position.

I say, "I'll take the one farthest to the right."

With that we watch as the flock commits to a return pass, the duck in the lead having completed its turn toward us, losing altitude in the process, dropping from its position of maybe 40 yards above the water to one that is only a few feet off the tops of the foam-covered waves.

I think: From a transportation point of view, some of these birds are in for a detour, their trip from the parklands of northern Canada, where they breed and spend the summer, to the Gulf of Mexico or maybe Chesapeake Bay or maybe Florida in danger of being interrupted in a very dramatic way.

"*Brrrrr, brrrrr.*"

The lead bird passes. As it does, without speaking Willy and I stand, shoulder our guns, and make our alignments, trying to swing with birds that now, having seen our movements, are banking hard away, clawing for altitude and swinging up and to their left, attempting to put as much wind beneath their wings as possible, beating the air at a pace that has essentially changed from metronomic to frantic.

I shoot the lead bird.

Rather, I shoot at it, missing. Then I squeeze the trigger again, this time trying to get far out in front of the bird, admittedly guessing somewhat wildly the distance I should lead it to effectively intersect its flight path.

Again I miss, and the duck, its tail completely turned from me, rises and rises still more, flying straight away, and safely.

I make another try with my third shot, picking out an alternate bird. But this volley also flies errant, as I knew it would. I haven't really recovered from the unrealized expectation that the lead bird was going to fold.

Willy, meanwhile, has killed cleanly the bird he had picked out.

Continuing a long-running joke between us, I say, "Why didn't you shoot?"

Then with a wave of a hand I send Chuck into the cold lake. I watch as he maneuvers along the slippery shoreline before submerging himself neck-deep in water, beginning his job of distinguishing between decoys and dead bird, swimming farther and farther out until, nearly at the end of our decoy string, he spots the bluebill, a drake, floating upside down to his left.

A third duck in the bag.

I relight my cigar.

Once again we wait.

A mechanic living in International Falls once told me a bad day of duck hunting is better than any day at work. There's truth here, because the number of birds seen or unseen, shot or not, in the end is only a marginal barometer of a duck hunt's success.

This is especially the case on Lake of the Woods, where the sound of a strong outboard cranking on a frigid morning, the smell of combusted gasoline rising with steamy exhaust, the excitement of dogs climbing into frost-laden boats, and the prospect of making big runs on big water, and doing it successfully, even in the dark, are the real attractions.

At sunset, as we douse the fire and begin toting gear to the boat, we have only three birds.

Still it was a good day.

Willy says, "Let's eat duck tonight."

"OK."

We push the boat into deep water, where I lower the motor and turn the key. The best outboard, I've always believed, is one that gets you home at the end of the day. When mine catches, I feel a sense of relief.

Then I maneuver the boat to the outer edge of our decoys, where Willy, employing an aluminum hook, picks up blocks while trying to fend off dogs, who, curious about the undertaking, are peering over the bow.

One by one, the fake little birds are recovered, their 20-foot cords wrapped around their keels, their soft lead anchors curled around their necks. Willy cups his hands to his mouth and says: "The water's cold. Really cold."

Then we stow the decoys in the bow and pull on all manner of bulbous clothing, including down and Gore-Tex® coats, heavy boots, thickly knit caps, hoods, face masks, even snowmobile helmets with plastic shields.

Knowing what's coming, the dogs curl tightly on the floor, amidships.

I flip on the running lights.

"Ready?" I yell through my knit balaclava and hood, drawn tightly against my face.

Willy nods.

I push the throttle forward. The engine howls as the boat struggles to get up on plane, our gear and the rolling waves contributing to an inertia that is difficult to overcome.

Willy holds the map in his hands. Each time I turn, I point to the spot on the map where I think we are, in effect confirming with Willy which dark island off the bow correlates to which dot on the map.

The wind, water, and darkness all contribute to a sense of vertigo, a feeling that the hauntingly dark shoreline and the occasional cabin on it, long closed for the season, are both real and unreal.

I think: Tonight we eat duck.

Tomorrow we do this again.

Empty Skies:
America's Ducks
in Crisis

Empty Skies: Ducks in Crisis

SUNDAY, FEBRUARY 7, 1988

Bayou LaFourche, LA—Major concentrations of North America's dwindling duck populations are being decimated by hunters in Louisiana, where state and federal agents estimate the annual illegal harvest of waterfowl is at least four times the number of ducks killed legally.

Interviews with agents, hunters, and others who live and work in the bayous of southeast Louisiana confirm that laws established to protect waterfowl are widely disregarded in Louisiana, which, with the possible exception of California, winters more ducks than any other state.

In addition, memoranda obtained by the *Pioneer Press* show that Fish and Wildlife Service officials in Washington, D.C., have known since at least 1970 the nature and scope of criminal activity in Louisiana involving ducks. But the service has not significantly increased the number of agents permanently assigned to Louisiana. Nor has it undertaken studies to determine the impact duck poaching in Louisiana or elsewhere has on the continent's waterfowl.

Officials of Ducks Unlimited, a 600,000-member conservation group, also have known of Louisiana waterfowl-hunting abuses since at least 1985, when *Ducks Unlimited* magazine senior editor Nicoletta Barrie traveled to Louisiana to document the problem. But officials of the organization refused to publish her story.

The abuses continue unabated. In the 1986–87 waterfowl season, federal and state agents apprehended in excess of 1,200 Louisiana hunters. Among them was Benny Cenac of Houma, Louisiana. A former Ducks Unlimited national trustee, Cenac had exceeded his daily limit of ducks.

"I wasn't one of the big duck killers in Louisiana, but I'll admit I never stopped at a limit from the time I was first taken hunting as a kid until I was caught. Nor did anyone I know," said Cenac, 32, who today is cooperating with federal game officials in a variety of hunter education programs.

The illegal harvest of ducks is particularly crucial in 1988 because populations of many duck species are at or near all-time lows (62 million now compared with 150 million in the 1940s), and because more habitat—upon which the future of waterfowl depends—now exists in the United States and Canada than there are ducks to fill it. Many waterfowl experts believe North America's ducks are at their most critical juncture in history.

Yet in the supplemental environmental impact statement prepared by the Fish and Wildlife Service before the nation's 1987 duck seasons, the service addressed the issue of illegal harvest of ducks only in passing. "No attempt to quantify illegal harvest is made," the report said. "It is assumed it is considerably less than the legal harvest and does not invalidate inferences and conclusions based on estimates of the legal harvest."

But in Louisiana, agents assigned to protect ducks say the season just concluded was among the state's worst for violations by hunters. Said Dave Hall, a Fish and Wildlife Service special agent who has worked in the Louisiana bayous for much of his nearly 30-year career: "I'd bet my life the total number of ducks killed each year in Louisiana is at least four times the reported estimated legal harvest. It may be a lot more.

"I wouldn't even want to estimate the number of ducks killed over the legal limit in Louisiana," said Louisiana state wildlife agent Roy Chauvin. "It would be piles and piles and piles."

Shooting lead instead of steel shot, hunting without licenses and stamps, using unplugged shotguns, baiting ducks with corn and milo, "creeping" up on geese to shoot them on the ground, and killing well in excess of legal limits are typical of violations found by agents in Louisiana in the 1987–88 season.

During the state's most recent 10-day September teal season, Fish and Wildlife Service special agent Bill Mellor of Metairie, Louisiana, on one day tagged seven hunters in possession of 192 ducks, including pintails and mottled ducks, which are protected during the teal season. The daily Louisiana duck limit is up to five, depending on the "point value" assigned the species of ducks in a hunter's bag.

Mellor found the daily limits grossly exceeded again on December 26, 1987, when he and other agents tagged three hunters with 71 ducks. Two weeks later, on January 9, 1988, Mellor and his colleagues tagged another three hunters with 168 ducks. Ninety of the birds were in the hunters' duck-camp refrigerator; 78 had been shot the morning of the arrest.

Yet another morning, a colleague of Mellor's arrested a hunter who had killed 53 ducks in a single outing.

"This year might have been a little worse than others, but not much," Mellor said. "If there was any difference between this season and others, it was that we couldn't hit some of the big baited areas as hard as we wanted to. Our plane was down for repairs and that inhibited our movement."

In all, during the 1987–88 season, Mellor placed 78 hunters under surveillance. Of these, 61 were tagged with a total of 130 violations. Of the 61 hunters arrested, 35 were over their limits, possessing, among them, 574 ducks.

Mellor wasn't the only agent in the marsh. Louisiana game warden Chauvin said the past duck season was the worst in terms of violations in his 14 years as a state employee, despite his and others' efforts to educate Louisiana hunters about the effects of overkill on ducks, which many observers believe have declined in Louisiana by 80 percent since the 1970s.

"Usually you have to work on someone to catch them violating duck laws," Chauvin said. "Granted, in Louisiana you don't have to work very hard, but usually you have to work at least a little hard. Not this year. This year, I didn't check a single legal duck hunter. The low point for me was one Sunday when I came home from church and heard shooting across the swamp from my backyard. I got in my pirogue [pronounced PEE-row—a type of canoe that is paddled or poled] and paddled over to see what was going on. There was a guy I knew. He had killed 20 ducks.

"I'd be lying to you if I said I don't get discouraged. Just once I'd like to go into a duck camp, find the hunters legal, and sit down with them to have a cup of coffee and talk about the marsh and the valuable experience duck hunting can offer."

Mellor and Chauvin caution that the enforcement methods they and other agents employ often focus on areas where ducks concentrate, and on areas where duck "outlaws," as they're known in Louisiana, tend to be. Consequently, the number of violators they contact may be disproportionately high relative to the number of violators among all Louisiana duck hunters.

Also, Mellor, Chauvin, and other agents say some Louisiana hunters commit serious waterfowl violations because they have the opportunity to commit them. "If hunters elsewhere had the same numbers of ducks available to them, they likely would violate the law as well," said Hall, who has spent much of his career observing hunter behavior in Louisiana and elsewhere.

Still, a pattern of almost wanton disregard for waterfowl regulations seems ingrained in the Louisiana culture. One federal agent, for example, Joe Oliveros of Monroe, Louisiana, observed a cross section of Louisiana duck hunters from "spy blinds" for three years before he saw a hunter who had the opportunity to exceed his limit but did not.

In years past, it was Cajuns—people who live in and among the

103

complicated maze of bayous and marshes off the Louisiana coast—who did most of the duck killing. Some of the birds were kept for eating. Others were given to friends and family. Still others were sold to restaurants in New Orleans and beyond.

Today, the Cajuns' overharvest of ducks, while serious, is far exceeded, according to state and federal agents, by the wealthier and oftentimes city-dwelling sportsmen who belong to the many duck clubs that have proliferated in recent years in Louisiana.

Non-residents—people from "up north"—also have been among the many duck hunters busted by state and federal agents for violating game laws. Sometimes these hunters are paid guests at commercial duck camps; sometimes they are invited guests at camps owned by corporations.

"This state's in a virtual economic depression now because the oil and gas industries have all but collapsed," said Hall. "But good God Almighty you should've seen things a few years back when oil and gas were really cooking. These big corporations would fly their business guests into Louisiana from all over the country, pour the bait [feed] to the ducks, and let 'em have at it."

Western Oceanic Inc. of Houma, Louisiana, an oil exploration company, was sponsoring such a hunt for its customers November 3, 1984, when federal and state agents arrived. The company and four of its employees eventually pleaded guilty in federal court in New Orleans to violating federal laws prohibiting the possession or transportation of wildlife. More than 75 ducks were killed on the trip.

In addition to other game-law violations, Western Oceanic had supplied its customers with fake Louisiana hunting licenses. In an unusual plea bargaining arrangement, the company agreed to make a professional quality video for use by wildlife managers. The reported cost: about $65,000. The subject: problems facing migratory waterfowl.

In a similar case, U.S. Magistrate Michaelle Wynne in December 1987 fined Robert Dan Gray, vice-president of OK Fishing & Rental

Tool Inc. of Houma, Louisiana, $1,500, and ordered Gray to spend 30 days in a halfway house and perform 208 hours of community service. The charge: baiting ponds so company employees and their guests could kill ducks. Gray's company was also fined $2,500. Baiting was outlawed in 1935.

Still another problem facing migratory waterfowl in Louisiana is the number of people who hunt.

In the three years spanning 1941–1944, Louisiana averaged an estimated 42,000 duck hunters. In 1986, the state had 100,000 hunters, according to the Fish and Wildlife Service.

The rise in the number of hunters coincides with a 60-percent decline in the estimated continental duck population, from 150 million to 62 million.

Moreover, the ducks in 1986 were considerably more concentrated than they were in 1941 due to the loss, according to wildlife officials, of more than 650 square miles of Louisiana coastal marsh. Modern hunters also have better and faster boats than their forerunners had. Consequently, they kill more ducks.

In 1986, the legal harvest of ducks in Louisiana was 1.2 million, or about 200,000 more than the average estimated number killed between 1941–1944.

What is worrisome to many waterfowl managers is that the 1.2 million ducks taken in 1986 were felled from a continental duck population that had declined by 60 percent from what it was in the early 1940s.

Gerald Voisin, district manager of The Louisiana Land and Exploration Co. of Houma, Louisiana, the state's largest private landowner, is in the marsh-leasing business.

"We own 650,000 acres of Louisiana coastal marsh," Voisin said. "In 1960, we had six small duck-hunting leases on our land. By the early '70s, every square inch of our intermediate-brackish and freshwater marsh was leased. Today, we have a total of 400 leases on our land, which includes about 50 percent of our saline marshes, with a 200-person wait-ing list."

Cenac, the past Ducks Unlimited national trustee, said: "Down here, no one lets a duck lease go once they have it. I don't care if the guy files bankruptcy or gets divorced, he finds a way to pay his lease."

A memorandum dated March 15, 1971, directed from Fish and Wildlife Service special agents then stationed in Louisiana to their su-periors in Atlanta and Washington, D.C., described the waterfowl poach-ing problem in detail.

"On Nov. 28, 29, and 30, 1969, we returned on patrol to the marshes south of Houma, Louisiana, in the district's helicopter. Wherever we observed duck hunters and concentrations of waterfowl, we randomly landed and made inspections.

"During these three days we landed to inspect 34 parties of duck hunters. Thirty-three of these parties were apprehended for exceeding the daily bag limit, and in addition many were found to have committed multiple offenses.

"Evidence of baiting was frequent in conjunction with flagrant over the limits. On each of these three days we filled the litters attached to each pontoon of the helicopter with seized ducks. We also filled the cockpit with additional burlap bags of seized waterfowl.

"On each of these mornings we were forced to discontinue our patrol and return to the airport where arrangements had to be made to dispose of these large numbers of seized waterfowl.

"Throughout the 1969 regular duck season, agents planned to con-centrate their efforts on clubs and individuals who were baiting and flagrantly disregarding bag limits. But a critical lack of operating funds necessitated the grounding of our helicopter. The subsequent loss of the helicopter on opening day of the second segment of the 1970 Louisiana waterfowl season greatly depreciated our ability to maintain surveillance . . . we were forced to direct our patrols to pirogues.

"On Dec. 8, 1970, we inspected approximately 30 duck-hunting clubs. One hundred percent of these clubs produced evidence of baiting."

In recent years, additional state and federal wildlife agents have been temporarily assigned to Louisiana and other southern states during duck season, but the basic contingent of resident federal agents—presently numbering seven—in Louisiana hasn't changed in three decades, according to Don Pfitzer, assistant Fish and Wildlife Service regional director for public affairs stationed in Atlanta.

Also, the helicopter lost in 1970 has never been replaced, although the service leased one for a few years in the late 1970s.

"As to our equipment, our lack of it in Louisiana is not by design. We're trying to give our agents in Louisiana every bit of support we can within our budget," Pfitzer said.

Ducks Unlimited executive vice president Matthew B. Connolly Jr. confirmed in a telephone interview from the organization's national headquarters in Long Grove, Illinois, last week that officials of the organization refused in 1986 to publish in its magazine a story detailing criminal waterfowl activity in Louisiana.

"The decision to scrub the story was done under a different administration," Connolly said. "When [Nicoletta Barrie] was assigned to go to Louisiana I was with Ducks Unlimited, and in fact I approved the assignment. I subsequently left the organization, and have returned only recently to it. Her article was scrubbed by the former administration. I don't know the reasons why.

"I will say we ran a story in the magazine in 1977 about hunter ethics. And my editorial in the magazine in the upcoming fall issue will deal with the same subject. There will also be a companion article on the subject in that issue. We feel the issue is very important."

Louisiana ranks eighth among states in Ducks Unlimited members with 21,167. In 1986, these members contributed $1.5 million to the conservation group, the ninth largest such sum contributed by any state.

One Louisiana Ducks Unlimited member is Pat Canulette, sheriff of St. Tammany Parish. Canulette is both an ardent and a legal duck hunter.

"In Louisiana there are countless hunters who don't learn the right way to hunt, and don't care to learn the right way," Canulette said. "In Louisiana, it's been like, 'You're the ace if you kill more ducks than I do.' It's always been a fact of life down here that you kill what you want.

"I taught my son how to hunt, and hunt right. We only shoot our limit, and we never shoot hens. But when my son goes to school down here on a Monday and tells his friends he only shot five ducks over the weekend, they laugh at him.

"They say, 'What do you mean, you only shot five ducks? Aren't you a good hunter? Isn't your lease any good?' Then they say, 'My dad and me, we killed 50 ducks last weekend.'

"People down here just figure this is their state and their ducks and they have a right to shoot what they want.

"I said to a guy once who told me he had shot 60 ducks. I said, 'What in the hell are you going to do with all those ducks?'

"He said: 'Nobody left me any buffalo to shoot. Why should I leave anyone any ducks?'"

Waterfowl lawbreakers opportunistic, entrenched

SUNDAY, FEBRUARY 7, 1988

Researchers and wildlife agents agree that violators of waterfowl laws are opportunistic, and that a certain percentage of duck hunters—no matter where they live—will shoot in excess of their limits if birds are abundant.

Each fall, for example, some Minnesota and Wisconsin waterfowl-law violators are caught by state and federal agents in their home states, as well as in other states and in Canada. But the fact that ducks and geese migrate through Minnesota and Wisconsin during the hunting season rather than stay in the region for months as they do in Louisiana and across the South oftentimes reduces the nature and severity of waterfowl violations in northern states, officers say.

"You don't very often catch a Minnesota duck hunter grossly over his limit of birds," said Bill Zimmerman, U.S. Fish and Wildlife Service assistant special agent in charge of the service's Region 3 headquarters at Fort Snelling. "What they do here if they're going to go over their limits, particularly south of the Twin Cities along the Mississippi River, is what we call 'double trip.'

"It amounts to shooting one limit of ducks, then returning to their camp or resort to stash them before going back to the blind to shoot another limit."

In a study undertaken in 1979, University of Wisconsin–La Crosse professor Robert Jackson found that waterfowl-law violators are younger than non-violators (27.75 years of age compared with 33.33 years), are more prone than non-violators to shoot trap or skeet, are more likely to belong to sportsmen's organizations, read technical waterfowl magazines, use retrievers, duck calls, and camouflaged boats, are more likely to prepare blinds, score higher on waterfowl identification tests, and are more skilled in bagging waterfowl.

Retriever owners may take some comfort in knowing violators' dogs are, according to the study, less well trained than those of non-violators.

Conditions that increased a hunter's tendency to violate, Jackson found, included hunting on one's own property, believing there wasn't much chance of getting caught, the fact that game was abundant, the fact that the season was about to close, and the fact that a hunter didn't believe a regulation was necessary.

"Our studies were done from spy blinds, from which we watched Wisconsin and Minnesota waterfowl hunters who didn't know they were being watched," Jackson said. "In the study, we found that one out of five violated a game law while being watched. The federal government has always put that figure at 5 percent, so our findings were significant.

"Later, when we followed up with personal interviews with hunters in their homes, and asked the question, 'Have you ever violated game laws?' the answer was yes, 85 percent of the hunters had. While we did not attempt to distinguish between accidental and purposeful violations, we know many such violations are accidental, such as the misidentification of a particular species of duck."

Fish and Wildlife Service special agents stationed in the Twin Cities last year coordinated a check of hunters and anglers traveling on Interstate 94 near Alexandria, Minnesota. Involved, in addition to the service, were the Minnesota Department of Natural Resources, as well as agents from North Dakota, Manitoba, and Montana.

On Monday, October 26, and Tuesday, October 27, agents erected a sign along the freeway instructing anglers and hunters to stop for inspection. A total of 132 vehicles carrying 250 hunters were stopped. Thirty-five hunters were cited as violators of game laws.

Of the 35 cited, 25 had violated waterfowl regulations. Laws broken included the transportation of birds without identifying plumage, exceeding the hen mallard limit, possession of protected canvasbacks, and possession of birds in excess of the limit.

Three of the overlimits were gross in nature, officers said, adding that most of the hunters were from the Twin Cities and Wisconsin.

Historically, laws governing the taking of fish and game in the United States have been socially acceptable to break, according to Fish and Wildlife Service special agent Dave Hall of Slidell, Louisiana.

In part, this is because many of America's early settlers poached game from large landowners in Europe. Many of them—and their forebears—had long been denied hunting and fishing rights due to social or economic class.

Despite the fact that in America laws were enacted that make wildlife the domain of the public, not landowners, "there's been a long tradition in this country that each of us has a right to all the fish and game we can get," Hall said.

Jackson noted in his study that traditions society deemed appropriate before the enactment of hunting regulations (the Migratory Bird Treaty Act was passed in 1918) don't necessarily change when game laws are enacted. Jackson also noted that behavior is an expression of the personality and values of an individual, as well as the groups with which he identifies.

"That's why if baiting ducks, roost-shooting wood ducks, and taking over the limit of ducks were practiced by a young hunter's role models, that's how he's going to learn to hunt," Hall said in a recent paper he presented on the subject, adding:

"Studies have shown that to raise a person from one level of ethical behavior to another level requires that the person become involved

111

with another person already at the higher level. But hunters at higher ethical levels are not always available. When they are, they often aren't persuasive enough to change the strong traditions that exist in some areas."

Federal agents in Louisiana believe strict enforcement of waterfowl laws by an expanded resident corps of well-equipped officers will play a major role in reducing the illegal harvest of ducks in the South.

But education about the effects of overharvest on the waterfowl population will play the largest role, they say.

"No one loves ducks and duck hunting more than a duck hunter," Hall said. "But, due to a variety of factors, habitat being the primary one, the birds are declining faster than hunting traditions in some parts of the country are changing.

"Psychologists say effective behavioral changes often occur during a crisis. With ducks, we're in a crisis now."

Hunters take ducks 'like their daddies did'

SUNDAY, FEBRUARY 7, 1988

Cut Off, LA—With the turn of a key, Jesse Duet, perhaps the most proficient waterfowl hunter in history, breathes life into the boat that will take him to his duck camp in the Louisiana bayous.

The boat, its twin exhaust stacks pointed skyward, lifts atop the water as Duet throttles gas into the big Chevy inboard. Trailing is a neat wake that angles smoothly from the transom before breaking against the hulls of docked shrimp boats.

The month is January. The time, 5:30 P.M. Save for the dim glow of dashboard lights silhouetting Duet's face, everything is black.

The route to the camp might confuse even some of Duet's fellow Cajuns. The interconnecting channels and canals that lace Louisiana's coastal marshes are so complex that they appear from an airplane like strands of spaghetti dropped atop a map. Even if the armed guard who watches the canal separating the town of Cut Off from Duet's camp could be circumvented, a man unfamiliar with the area could never successfully navigate these tangled waterways.

Which is how Duet likes it. The camp has been home to him since he was a kid, and he has used it as a base to kill thousands and thousands and thousands and thousands of ducks—more ducks than most hunters see in a lifetime.

"When I was young I would sometimes shoot a case of shells a day,"

113

Duet will tell you. In a case, there are 500 shotgun shells.

Duet's propensity to align the bead of his shotgun with the path of a passing duck does not make him unique in Louisiana. Here, duck hunting is a sacrosanct exercise, and many hunters—they are nearly all men—gauge their virility by the number of birds bagged in a day. The equation is simple: the more birds, the better the man.

Duet cannot remember linking one with the other as a kid. Duck hunting was simply something he did because his friends and family needed ducks to eat. Unable to speak English until he was 18 (like many Cajuns, his native tongue is French), Duet spent his youth in the marsh, catching bullfrogs, trapping muskrats, picking off a 'gator now and then—and shooting ducks.

A half-hour passes before Duet cuts the engine to idle and steers the boat into a shed already flush with three boats. Two are mudboats, capable of running in water only inches deep; the other is an outboard-rigged johnboat.

"Come in," Duet says to a visitor, fending off an assortment of cats and black Labradors, the camp's other permanent residents. "Bring your gear. I'll make dinner."

Most evenings, dinner for Duet consists of duck or fish. This evening, it's fish—red fish—half of it baked Cajun style, the other half barbecued on a gas grill outside.

"I'll tell you how in my life I have killed ducks," Duet says as he spices the fish in a manner a Northerner might consider excessive. "I have killed more than my share, I admit that, and I'm not proud of it. I hunt legal now. But not everybody does in Louisiana. And with the duck population down the way it is, that's a problem."

Duet begins by describing how he and others in Louisiana's marsh communities learned from their daddies how to kill ducks and other birds, and how their daddies learned from their daddies.

"During the season, limits didn't mean much to us," he said. "We just shot what we wanted to shoot. I myself have never sold a duck, but a lot of people did. Ducks I couldn't eat or my friends couldn't eat, I just gave away.

"In addition to hunting during the season, we also hunted after the season. In fact, that's when most of us hunted, because the birds don't have as many pinfeathers then. Ask a Cajun and he'll tell you that after the season is the best time to hunt ducks.

"In spring, when the teal come back from Mexico and South America, that's another good time to hunt. There are lots of ducks around at the time, and they are already paired up, ready to begin breeding up north. When I was younger we'd also shoot night herons, ibises, and egrets. It was herons we preferred most. Egrets were the least of our favorites. But we would eat them on occasion.

"Then, in July, mottled ducks would gather in these marshes. They also provided good shooting. Later, in September, the teal would start arriving from up north. The season would open, and we'd start all over again."

None of this was out of the ordinary. Nearly everyone in the marsh did it and spoke freely of it, oftentimes bragging openly about how many ducks they killed in how short a time. Game wardens weren't much of a problem, not when Duet was a kid. Especially not those employed by the state of Louisiana.

"When I was young, if a north wind came through, we'd always get lots of new ducks in the marsh," Duet recalled. "Every time that wind blew, I'd go out and kill 50 or 60 ducks. I knew two wardens would be waiting for me when I got back to camp. I also knew they'd take half my ducks for themselves and leave half for me."

Duet was able to kill more ducks than most Cajuns because he was a better duck hunter than most Cajuns. His methodology was better, too. Long after live decoys were outlawed in 1935, he used them to attract wild birds to within gun range. Nothing, he said, was more effective for killing ducks.

"Ducks just love to come into live decoys," Duet said. "I didn't

AN HOUR BEFORE DAWN

even know they were illegal until about 25 years ago when a relative got caught using them."

Jesse Duet has never met Dennis Treitler, who lives and traps east of Duet's duck camp, in the lowlands on the other side of the Mississippi River. But the men have one thing in common: a love of ducks and duck hunting.

In January, during trapping season, Treitler can be found most mornings beginning at about 4:00 A.M. at a roadside cafe in St. Bernard Parish. The cafe is run by a friend of Treitler's whose nickname is Bozo. Before heading into the marsh to check his traps, Treitler often stops at Bozo's place for breakfast—a quart Mason jar filled with iced Coca-Cola.

A square-shouldered man with fists as big as anvils and energy to burn, Treitler is the son of a son of a duck hunter. He grew up in Bayou Bienvenue, where boats were used for transportation. As a kid, he routinely ate raccoon and muskrat, in addition to ducks. He still does.

"When they grow up, some kids want to be firemen, lawyers, or doctors," Treitler said. "I grew up wanting to be a duck hunter." One year, Treitler, his two brothers, his uncle, and two nephews won every major duck-calling contest in Louisiana.

Now 41 years old and a legal hunter for the past "six or eight" years, Treitler freely admits he's done a lot of "violating" and "outlawing."

"I did a lot that was illegal, I know it," he said. "I learned to outlaw from my dad, who was a mink trapper in the flooded cyprus swamps and a market hunter of ducks for several prominent restaurants in New Orleans. Even though market hunting was illegal at the time, that's what Dad did. Every day, when he went into the marsh, he had to kill 'X' ducks, and he stayed until he killed them. It wasn't like he was breaking the law or anything. It was like going to the office. It was just our way of life. Like everyone else in Louisiana, we grew up thinking it was acceptable.

"When I was a kid, there were so many ducks, you never, ever thought the resource would run out. It was a common thing for my dad and I to go into the marsh with 1,500 shells for a morning's shoot. Some days we'd get 60 or 70 birds. Other days we'd get 200, 300, 400, whatever.

"This went on for years, until finally we started seeing some of our friends get caught by federal agents. We figured then we'd better watch our step. The last real big outlaw hunt I made with Dad was when I was 16 years old (in 1963). We killed 300 ducks in one day. The season was closed at the time."

Neither Treitler nor his father was caught violating game laws in Louisiana. But other violators Treitler knew were caught. Some years ago, that began to worry him. Something else worried him, too: the drastic decline in ducks Louisiana—and the nation—has experienced in recent decades.

"I'm not afraid of being caught violating," Treitler said. "I'm afraid of no man, federal agent or not. But there aren't 20 percent of the ducks down here that there were just 10 years ago. And with the loss of habitat the way it is in the North and South, combined with the illegal kill by hunters, things don't look too good for the birds.

"What made me change was this: I want to save the ducks. When you see ducks in the trouble they are, something's got to give. You look at the situation and if you're a violator, you're either going to be a man about it and do something good. Or you're going to be an asshole and keep violating. In my case, I chose to be a man."

Benny Cenac of Houma, Louisiana, differs from Treitler in at least two ways. One, Cenac is wealthy. Two, Cenac last year was caught violating state and federal game laws. The offense: He finished a morning shoot with too many ducks in his possession.

Catching Cenac, a friendly, forthright man and past national Ducks Unlimited trustee, was no easy chore for state wildlife agent Roy Chauvin and federal special agent Bill Mellor, in large part because Cenac's hunting club is massive, measuring 30,000 acres and boasting 100 deer stands and 36 duck blinds, as well as a handful of dove fields. The electronically operated gate at the camp entrance complicated matters even further for the agents.

Still, Chauvin and Mellor one morning were hiding in the swamp on the grounds of Cenac's camp when Cenac stashed a bag of ducks that put him over his daily limit. They had their man.

A year later, on a cool morning in January 1988, Cenac talked about duck hunting, Louisiana style.

"I was 6 years old when I first went duck hunting," Cenac said. "I'm 32 years old now. In that time, I can't remember stopping shooting when I reached a legal limit of ducks. Nor in that time did I know anyone who did. In Louisiana, it's just tradition. You shoot like you want, what you want, when you want until you get tired of shooting. Down here, everyone, rich or poor, has a duck camp. Up north, it may just be rich people. Down here, most everyone has one. It's just a way of life to shoot the number of ducks you want to shoot.

"But in recent years, we were cutting back what we shot here at the camp. We had just been shooting what amounted to a legal limit for everyone in camp, meaning that if the limit was five, we'd see to it that five ducks were shot for each hunter in camp. We weren't big killers. What we were doing was wrong, I admit that, because it's illegal to party-hunt ducks. On occasion over the years we might have killed maybe 10, 15, 20 ducks a morning apiece. But we weren't big killers, not like a lot of people."

For his offense, Cenac was placed on a year's probation and agreed in a plea bargain to contribute $10,000 to hunter education programs. In exchange, he retained his hunting rights.

Cenac is now cooperating with federal game officials, trying to educate Louisiana hunters about the decline of ducks and the impact he believes illegal overharvest has on waterfowl.

Cenac concedes, however, that changing traditions in Louisiana is a tall order.

"Down here in the bayous, they live to 'pass the good time' as we say. They kill an animal or two at night with a bull eye [spotlight], invite a few people over, have a few drinks—and pass the good time," Cenac said.

"It's not that Louisiana people don't care about their natural resources, they do. It's not that they're stupid, either. Many of them just don't know any better. No one ever told them the ducks they're shooting represent the major concentrations of ducks in North America."

At 5:30 A.M., Jesse Duet shuffles into the kitchen of his duck camp to prepare breakfast. Outside, the wind blows hard off the Gulf of Mexico, stirring whitecaps on open stretches of the marsh. A short time passes before Duet calls to a visitor. "Breakfast is ready," he says.

Soon Duet is out the door and loading decoys and other hunting supplies into his boat. Then he guides the boat across the canal in front of his camp, where he transfers the gear to a high-powered mudboat. With a roar, the mudboat's engine is started, and the visitor climbs aboard.

"The ducks will fly this morning," Duet says, the mudboat operating unhindered in water only 12 inches deep. "This wind will push them around."

Duet is not often mistaken when the subject is ducks, and this morning is no exception.

Gadwall. Wigeon. Pintails. Blue-winged teal. Mallards.

By sunrise, each is aloft, flying in no particular direction, playing the harsh Louisiana wind in a manner only ducks can.

Duck agents battle long odds

MONDAY, FEBRUARY 8, 1988

In the Louisiana Bayous—Six A.M. U.S. Fish and Wildlife Service special agent Bill Mellor has been out of bed three hours. Standing at the console of his 16-foot-long Boston Whaler, power cut to its 150-horsepower engine, Mellor listens as waves slap against the craft's fiberglass hull. Otherwise, the morning is still.

With Mellor are Fish and Wildlife Service special agent George Hines of Columbia, South Carolina, and South Carolina state wildlife agent Tommy Haile. The two have been assigned to help Mellor enforce waterfowl laws during Louisiana's duck season.

Without warning, the report of a shotgun is heard in the distance, the fifth in as many minutes.

"That's the 11th shot that guy's fired," Mellor says. "Whoever it is, he's over his limit by now."

For Mellor and his fellow agents, getting to the culprit won't be easy, but it's important that they do. They believe it is illegal overharvest—widespread in Louisiana—that is one of the problems threatening North America's dwindling duck population.

Complicating enforcement of the regulations is a Louisiana coast buffered by a band of marshes that stretches farther than the eye can see, in some places 40 miles or more. Interwoven among these watery grasslands are canals, some private, some public, that angle in every imaginable direction.

Most of the canals are deep enough to run an outboard motor. But the marshes must be traversed by either pirogue or mudboat, which is a craft powered by an inboard engine and capable of operating in water only inches deep.

Stacked in Mellor's boat are three pirogues, which agents use to sneak on hunters suspected of running afoul of the law.

Mellor starts the outboard and pushes the engine throttle forward. As he does, the boat, the pirogues, and the agents are thrust ahead, first at 20 mph, then 30, then 40. The boat tops out at a speed in excess of 50 mph, its hull barely in the water as it skims atop the marsh, the big outboard hanging on the transom, screaming.

When he approaches an intersecting canal, Mellor cranks the boat's steering wheel hard left, changing the craft's direction 90 degrees. He's guessing now where the hunter might be. This time he gets lucky. In the middle of the canal, crossing from one marsh to another, is a young man in a pirogue.

Riveting his eyes on the man, Mellor cuts the engine and the Whaler settles into the water with a *whoosh*. Sometimes a hunter possessing too many ducks will make a move that gives him away. Mellor watches. And waits. As he does, the man in the pirogue quickens his pace in an attempt to reach the adjacent marsh.

Mellor's response is instant: He guns the outboard and places the bow of the Whaler to within inches of the pirogue.

Checkmate.

"Hold it right there. Game wardens," Mellor says.

For a wildlife agent, this is the trickiest part. The hunter has a gun, that much is certain. Violator or not, the hunter usually will not make a threatening move. But all wildlife agents are cautious nonetheless.

Hines says: "I'd like to take a look at that gun. And we'll need to see your license."

Taking the man's rusty weapon, Hines checks to see if it is "plugged"

121

so it can hold only three shells. It is. Then he looks at the license. Again, everything is in order.

Mellor, meanwhile, inspects the man's ducks—he has four—then says, "That steel shot you're using?"

"I got some steel," the man says. "I got some lead."

Mellor suspects the man is lying. "Let's see all your shells," he says. Using a magnet, he determines quickly all the shells are lead.

"You don't have any steel," Mellor says.

"I tried to buy some," the man says. "I couldn't. All the stores were out."

Meanwhile, Haile, the South Carolina state agent, spots two other men crossing the marsh in a pirogue. Determining they are friends of the man they have stopped (even though the man said he was alone), and that the hunters are returning to the group's camp, Haile and Hines take Mellor's boat to head them off. Mellor, meanwhile, stays behind to write the stopped hunter a ticket for possession of lead shot.

The two men in the pirogue are found, as was their friend, to be using only lead-shot shells. Otherwise, they are legal. Hines and Haile make a mental note, however, that a shed at their camp contains bags of corn. It's a virtual certainty the men had been baiting ducks. It's also likely, the agents say, that the hunters stashed in the marsh excess ducks from their morning shoot.

The encounter ends when the agents seize all 12 of the hunters' ducks. Felled by lead shot, they were taken illegally. They must be forfeited.

"Three guys checked, three guys busted," Mellor says later. "Another morning in the marsh."

To be a duck cop in Louisiana, it helps if you have an aversion to sleep. During most of the more than 60 days waterfowl can be legally hunted in Louisiana, agents rise at two or three every morning and oftentimes aren't in bed until after midnight.

That's the easy part.

The hard part includes sneaking by armed guards that protect some violators' duck camps; lying in alligator-infested, mosquito-infested, gnat-infested, water-moccasin–infested marshes many mornings from 4:00 A.M. until hunters come to their blinds about 6:30 A.M., then lying in the marsh for up to five more hours documenting the hunters' actions; confronting armed hunters in the field, some of whom "make a break for it" into the bayou; flying in airplanes in bad weather, the same conditions that put ducks to wing.

For the last 10 years or so, because of budget restraints, federal agents assigned to Louisiana have been flying in fixed-wing aircraft, not helicopters.

"Baiting is a real big problem down here," says the 37-year-old Mellor, a pilot-agent. "We've been cracking down on it as hard as we can, and we're making some progress. But it's difficult to do without a helicopter. When the service had a helicopter in Louisiana back in the '70s, we were able to hold the baiting more in check."

Fish and Wildlife Service special agent Dave Hall of Slidell, Louisiana, agrees the helicopter "put the fear of God" in Louisiana waterfowl-law violators.

"There are so many helicopters down here, the hunters couldn't tell which ones belonged to the oil and gas companies and which one was ours," Hall said. "The advantage the helicopter gave us was this: When we were in the air and we saw bait in the water (corn especially is easy to spot from above), we just came down on the bait and apprehended the hunters—if the bait was being hunted at the time.

"On occasion, the hunters would try to make a break for it. We had a bullhorn mounted underneath the chopper that was amplified. When we dropped out of the sky, we simply identified ourselves as special agents and told the hunters not to move. If they were smart, they didn't."

Without a helicopter, catching violators who bait ducks is considerably more difficult.

123

"When we fly our airplane (a Super Cub) over the marsh, we take a lot of aerial photographs," Mellor said. "We have the photographs blown up and mark on them the location of the hunters' blinds, their camp, and where we saw the bait.

"We then hold a meeting of all agents who will be included in the operation. An entry route into the area is determined. The route must get us by any guards the hunters may have hired to watch for us. Each agent is given an assignment. We figure out who will go where and at what time."

On the first morning of the operation, one or more agents sneak into the violators' marsh and "steal" some of the bait. Agents need this to make a conviction stick.

"It's illegal to hunt a baited area within 10 days of putting bait out," Mellor said. "But ducks like bait so much, they eat it in a hurry. So we would be taking a chance if we didn't go after the bait as soon as possible. We have 10 days to get the hunters, who might not come out to their camp until the weekend. But we've got to get the bait sample right away, before the ducks eat it."

On the second night of the operation, agents stack three or four pirogues into a high-powered boat and head into the marsh. The idea is to get the motorboat as close to the baited area as possible, then use the pirogues to position the agents near the hunters' blinds.

"Usually our intelligence is pretty good, so we have pretty good knowledge about when an area is going to be hunted. But people's plans change. If we're out there and for some reason the hunters decide not to hunt that day, we have to come back the next night. From the time we took the bait as evidence, we have 10 days to catch someone hunting the area. We'll come back 10 times in a row if that's what it takes to catch someone."

The Fish and Wildlife Service stations seven of its approximately 180 special agents in Louisiana. In addition to waterfowl laws, agents are charged with enforcing interstate wildlife transportation laws (the

Lacey Act), the Endangered Species Act, the Airborne Hunting Act, and all other federal laws regulating wildlife, including fish.

"Seven agents doesn't come close to what they need down here," said Benny Cenac of Houma, Louisiana, who was pinched by Mellor and Louisiana state wildlife agent Captain Roy Chauvin a year ago for exceeding his daily limit of ducks. "If they had one agent in each parish [county] it wouldn't be enough."

The state of Louisiana also employs wildlife agents. Like federal agents, state agents are charged with enforcing waterfowl laws. But the latters' jobs oftentimes are politically vulnerable, observers say, if they nab the wrong person.

Louisiana state agent Chauvin doesn't play that game.

"In Louisiana, everything's political," he said. "If you're a state agent, you've got to be strong to remain unaffected by it. It's always been OK in Louisiana to pinch the little man, the poor man who doesn't have friends in the right places. But you pinch someone who knows a legislator or whomever, and they'll try to get to you.

"In my job, I should be free from political interference, but that's not the way of life. I've seen good wildlife agents come and go. They performed their job well, but they couldn't take the pressure. It's not easy to do your job if you're worrying that the person you catch violating game laws is the 'wrong' person—a county attorney or whoever."

Chauvin won't talk about it, but his friends and colleagues say he and his family have paid a price for his no-politics, protect-the-resource attitude.

"I've been run over in my boat, left for dead in the marsh in the middle of the night, and I've been shot at a couple of times," Chauvin said. "But it doesn't matter to me who I catch. Sometimes after I catch some big-name guy I get a phone call from people in the 'right' places. They say, 'Do you know who you caught?' I tell them, 'Yea, I know, and I don't care.' I tell them if it was Ronald Reagan coming across the levee with too many ducks, I'd bust him.

"They say I'm a purist, that I should be working somewhere else. Well, I don't think so. My decisions are based on what's good for wildlife. That's first. Second come the 'good' people who hunt, the ones who don't violate. They need my help protecting the resource. Third comes the department I work for.

"I'll be the first to admit I got my job through politics. All state wildlife agents down here do. But that doesn't affect how I do my job. We have a lot of good people who work for our department. I think it could become unpoliticized. Deep down, a lot of people in the department want to do it. The question is, who's going to be the first to stand up and sacrifice their career?

"I know regarding ducks we better get it together pretty soon. I've noticed a serious decline in the birds in the last 10 years. I don't think it's bottomed out, either.

"We've got to stop violators, and we've got to educate people about caring for wildlife. But it's not easy. None of it's easy. Do you know how hard it is to catch violators behind armed guards? We do it, but it's hard. I tell those people, 'You want to kill all the ducks, go ahead and kill them all. But when they're all gone, don't be calling me.'

"Something's got to change. You catch people with 58 ducks, 85 ducks, 102 ducks, shooting doves over bait, shooting ducks over bait. Some of these people I've already caught once. Somebody ain't getting the message.

"I don't know what it'll take to wake these people up. When the last damn duck flies over Louisiana, maybe that'll do it.

"If that happens, I just hope everyone doesn't rush to get their guns to shoot it.

"I'd be embarrassed."

EMPTY SKIES: AMERICA'S DUCKS IN CRISIS
Camera in hand, agent tells story

MONDAY, FEBRUARY 8, 1988

New Orleans—Louisiana may be the only state in the nation where the guy who busts you for violating game laws also offers you a movie deal.

This is particularly likely if Dave Hall, U.S. Fish and Wildlife Service special agent, is the man flashing the badge.

Much to the frustration and embarrassment of many of his Fish and Wildlife Service colleagues, Hall is going public in a big way with what he believes is a major factor affecting North American waterfowl—illegal kill.

"I've been making the case that illegal kill is a major problem affecting waterfowl for a long time," Hall said. "But for the 20 or more years I've been addressing the subject and trying to get people to face up to it, I haven't made a lot of progress. Meanwhile, ducks have continued to decline, mostly because of habitat loss, but illegal kill is hurting them, too.

"My career with the service is nearing its end, and in the recent past I've tried to evaluate my work to see what, if any, impact I've had on waterfowl in my 30 years with the service. To be honest, I guess I really haven't been too successful in changing attitudes. I'm not speaking so much of violators' attitudes, because even they know that what they're doing is affecting the resource.

"I'm talking about the attitudes of some of the biologists in Washington, D.C., and elsewhere who manage these birds. No matter what you tell them about what is happening in the field, they won't listen if you carry a badge. That's the way it's always been. If you're an enforcement officer, they don't listen. Even though I am a trained biologist, the badge seems to negate whatever contributions I and other agents try to make on the subject of illegal overkill of ducks."

Now Hall, recipient of the National Wildlife Federation's 1987 Achievement Award in the government category, has taken a new and innovative approach to telling his story. Working closely with U.S. magistrates in New Orleans, he has gained the cooperation of Louisiana game-law violators in his effort to educate Southern waterfowl hunters and Washington, D.C., biologists about the errors of their ways.

Which is how Hall became a movie mogul.

"One of the companies we busted for illegal overkill 'agreed' to loan me film-making equipment so I could put some of my violator friends on film and let them tell their stories for themselves," Hall said. "One of the smartest things I ever did was go back to the violators and say, 'Boys, we're in trouble with the ducks. You're going to have to help me save them by being honest with me on film about what you've been doing. Maybe then we can convince people about the severity of the situation.'"

"No problem," said the violators.

Thus, on any given day, Hall is in the Louisiana backwaters holding a camera and asking questions.

Hall: "How long have you been violating game laws?"

Violator: "My daddy's dad killed thousands of ducks each year, my daddy killed thousands of ducks each year, and for many years I killed thousands of ducks each year."

Hall: "Why'd you stop killing so many ducks?"

Violator: "Because it's wrong. Because there aren't many ducks left. And because if I don't stop, and if other violators don't stop, my children and their children won't have the same opportunities I've had in the marsh to see ducks."

Hall: "So illegal overkill of ducks is hurting the resource?"

Violator: "Anyone who says it isn't ought to be waiting tables somewhere, not managing ducks."

To many people it's dirty laundry that shouldn't be aired. They say it makes hunters look bad. They say it makes the Fish and Wildlife Service look bad, too.

"One of my biggest frustrations has been that the issue of illegal kill is so scary to some people that no matter what documentation you present, it's like, 'We don't want to hear it.'

"They worry, for instance, about anti-hunters and what they will say when they hear about the illegal kill. I tell them if hunters clean up their ranks they have nothing to fear from anyone. The record is clear: Hunters are the reason this country has as much wildlife as it does.

"Beyond that, in the process of saving ducks or any resource, it's not always in the cards to be a good guy who's liked by everyone. Some in the Fish and Wildlife Service think I'm uncontrollable, a loose cannon.

"Maybe I am. But what I'm doing is right for the resource and ultimately right for the duck hunter."

Minnesota aids Louisiana duck hunters

TUESDAY, FEBRUARY 9, 1988

Slidell, LA—When the 1987 Minnesota waterfowl season opened October 3, many blue-winged teal living on lakes near Bill Scott's home in Ely had already flown to Louisiana and points south.

Likewise with a sizable portion of blue-wings reared near Doug Lovander's home outside Willmar.

Among the earliest of migrating waterfowl, blue-winged teal each year fly south by the thousands, weeks, and in some instances months, before the Minnesota duck season opens.

For which hunters in Louisiana, Arkansas, Mississippi, Missouri, Iowa, and Illinois, among others, are forever grateful. Unlike Minnesota, these states usually sponsor special September teal seasons.

Louisiana hunters are also thankful their counterparts in Minnesota are denied late-season opportunities to hunt bluebills, one of the last ducks to fly south. More birds are thus left for the special January bluebill season Louisiana waterfowl managers tack onto the end of their regular season.

Louisiana's special teal and bluebill seasons underscore disparities that exist among waterfowl management plans in the Mississippi Flyway, of which Minnesota and Louisiana are members. The seasons also underscore the fact that Minnesota Department of Natural Resources waterfowl managers are among the most conservative in the United

States, while their Louisiana counterparts are among the most liberal.

The seasons also help explain why the average Louisiana duck hunter harvests more than twice the number of ducks a Minnesota hunter harvests. (In 1986, the legal estimated seasonal harvest per Louisiana hunter was 12. For Minnesota hunters, it was 5.94.)

Not accounted for in Minnesota–Louisiana harvest comparisons is the number of birds taken in excess of allowable limits, especially in Louisiana, which, with the possible exception of California, winters more ducks than any other state. Some state and federal agents in Louisiana say the illegal harvest there exceeds by at least four times the estimated legal harvest.

The illegal harvest, the agents say, represents a major threat to North America's dwindling duck population.

"It's difficult to say how many hunters take in excess of their limits during the special season," said Fish and Wildlife Service special agent Dave Hall. "Certainly a number do. But I don't believe a great number of non-target species are taken during the September teal season in Louisiana. There just aren't that many other species down here at the time.

"In fact, one of the good things the teal season does in Louisiana is limit, for the most part, the kill to teal, which are a relatively abundant species. By doing this, the out-of-season hunting that likely would occur in Louisiana at the time is negated. Come September, people down here want a taste of duck, and by having a teal season, the potential negative impact on other species in minimized."

That was not the case, however, one day during Louisiana's most recent September teal season when Fish and Wildlife Service special agent Bill Mellor of Metarie, Louisiana, and other agents apprehended seven hunters in possession of 192 ducks, including protected pintails and mottled ducks.

In addition to bonus seasons for scaup and teal, among other species, the Fish and Wildlife Service offers some states other options designed to maximize hunting opportunity. Options include bonus birds, split seasons, and zoning.

Minnesota takes advantage of none of these. Louisiana, on the other hand, utilizes bonus seasons for teal and bluebills, and splits the state into two zones. The western part of the state is in the Central Flyway; the eastern in the Mississippi.

The split allows western Louisiana to be governed by Central Flyway regulations, which are more liberal than those of the Mississippi Flyway.

Roger Holmes, Minnesota Department of Natural Resources wildlife section chief, represents the state on the Mississippi Flyway Council, which meets annually to propose season lengths and bag limits to the Fish and Wildlife Service.

"At flyway council meetings, everyone from the various states is pretty much vying for more hunting opportunity," Holmes said. "Split seasons. Bonus birds. Bonus seasons. Most states take whatever the Fish and Wildlife Service gives them. We don't. We're generally considered the most conservative managers in the nation from a natural resources viewpoint, especially from a waterfowl viewpoint.

"Among reasons we don't take any options is the fact that we have so many duck hunters (132,000 in 1986 compared with Louisiana's 100,000). We feel if we extend hunting opportunity too far, there's a chance we could cut into our breeding populations. We rank third or fourth in the nation in terms of ducks raised in the state, and we feel an obligation to protect these birds.

"This same kind of conservative approach to duck management is found across the northern states and Canada."

Holmes added that Minnesota restricts, rather than expands, duck-hunting opportunities, by delaying shooting until noon on opening day.

"This way we protect the birds more than we would if we allowed shooting to begin one-half hour before sunrise, as is the case the remainder of the season," Holmes said.

Minnesota also closes shooting at 4:00 P.M. on the opener and for

132

two weeks of the season thereafter.

"This provides birds with a feeding and resting period," Holmes said. "It's designed to protect the birds. It's also designed to hold migrating birds in the state longer than might otherwise be the case if shooting were allowed until sunset.

"Also, the 4:00 P.M. closing shifts hunting pressure to the migrants and away from our breeding birds, which we've found are harvested at a higher rate than migrators."

The Fish and Wildlife Service will not allow Minnesota or any duck-breeding state to hold September teal seasons. But Minnesota could implement a "bonus bluebill" rule, which after a certain date would allow a hunter to take his legal daily limit of four birds, as well as two extra bluebills.

"But we've long had the view in this state," said Holmes, "that four ducks a day is enough. We don't feel that to give duck hunters in Minnesota a good experience afield we have to increase the number of ducks they take.

"Besides, the bluebill bonus-bird system likely would increase violations among hunters, because ring-necked ducks would still be in the state at the time, and they can easily be mistaken for bluebills.

"Likely as not, it would also increase the take of species other than bluebills, because if a hunter were sitting in his blind with, say, four bluebills—the legal limit now—and two mallards came into his decoys, he might be tempted to shoot the two mallards. If he wasn't caught by a conservation officer doing it, he would legally be in possession of the proper number of birds, even though without the bonus the two mallards wouldn't have been shot."

Hugh Bateman, Louisiana Department of Wildlife and Fisheries wildlife biologist, is that state's representative to the Mississippi Flyway Council.

Bateman said that Louisiana is continuing its quest to be repositioned completely from the Mississippi Flyway to the Central Flyway.

133

Any change requires approval by the Fish and Wildlife Service.

Louisiana waterfowl managers believe the majority of ducks wintering in the state arrive via the Central Flyway, Bateman said, and that proper management of the birds dictates Louisiana therefore be governed by Central Flyway regulations.

He conceded, however, that Central Flyway waterfowl-hunting regulations are more liberal than Mississippi Flyway regulations, and that this factor is a determinant in the state's request to be moved from one flyway to the next.

"Historically, bag limits and season lengths have been more liberal in the Central Flyway, and that's one reason we want to change," Bateman said, noting that the Central Flyway portion of Louisiana enjoyed a 45-day duck season this year, while the Mississippi Flyway portion was restricted to 40 days (exclusive of bonus teal and bluebill seasons).

"Obviously, the more liberal regulations of the Central Flyway would be attractive to our hunters. But from a manager's viewpoint, we believe a state should be managed the same way other states in its majority flyway are managed. And the majority of our birds come from the Central Flyway." (Fish and Wildlife Service officials in Washington, D.C., dispute this, saying data on the subject are inconclusive.)

Asked whether increased hunter opportunity afforded by the more liberal Central Flyway regulations would compound Louisiana's illegal harvest problem, Bateman said:

"Illegal kill is something that needs to be addressed. There's need for improvement in Louisiana as there is in all areas of the country. You can't have a successful management plan unless you control illegal take.

"But I've heard these scare stories about things being out of control down here, and I think it's a bunch of garbage. I admit I'm pretty sensitive to people from other places shaking fingers and saying you ought to do this and you ought to do that. I don't think the illegal kill factor is as bad as a lot of people think.

"Habitat is what we need for ducks. That's what's important."

134

Rollin Sparrowe is the Fish and Wildlife Service's top waterfowl manager in Washington, D.C. Each summer, he and his staff digest requests and recommendations made by the four flyway councils—Atlantic, Mississippi, Central, Pacific—and produce a waterfowl-hunting framework.

In a telephone interview last week, Sparrowe said bonus birds, bonus seasons, and zoning options likely will continue to be offered by the service.

"We monitor these options and their effects on the resource," he said. "Many of the special seasons kill an insignificant number of ducks. A lot of them are not having an impact on the population."

Some in the Fish and Wildlife Service disagree. Among them are some of Sparrowe's subordinates who claim the service "has given away the store to the states at the flyway council meetings."

"The service isn't running the show anymore," said one biologist who asked not to be named. "What the service does these days at flyway council meetings is broker hunter opportunity between states. Iowa gets this, so Illinois gets that. What's best for the birds oftentimes comes last.

"Illinois, for example, has got themselves zoned into so many zones that they now have, in effect, multiple opening days. On paper that might not look so bad, but in reality what happens is this.

"The state's best hunters typically are the state's most mobile ones as well, and no matter where they live in the state they'll get to the different zones for each of the zone openers. Consequently, rather than having 'X' pressure on the birds in a certain area, you have 'X' plus all other people who come from surrounding areas. The same occurs for each zone opening.

"In addition, the majority of bird hunters, whether they are waterfowl or upland bird hunters, hunt only on opening day. This is because they have only marginal interest, because they can only get away from their families for a given amount of time each fall. Or, most important, because many of them are not skilled enough to take birds except on

135

opening day, when birds are less wary than they otherwise are in later season.

"Zoning, therefore, allows these less-skilled hunters not one opportunity at opening-day birds, but multiple opportunities.

"This is just one example of season aberrations that are being allowed in the interest of expanded hunting opportunity. Don't get me wrong, hunting-opportunity expansion is not bad when we have the ducks. Right now, we don't have the ducks."

Sparrowe stresses that "the service is still running the show" at flyway council meetings.

"The service will make the decisions necessary to manage the birds properly. Whether more restrictions are necessary remains to be answered. If bird populations require it, it can be done."

Regarding illegal kill, particularly in the southern wintering states, Sparrowe added, "We are actively considering the need for measuring this as one of our aspects of planning."

Erosion creates
a wildlife disaster

WEDNESDAY, FEBRUARY 10, 1988

Cut Off, LA—When the two met, Dave Hall descended on Jesse Duet like an angel from heaven.

"The wind was blowing hard off the gulf, real hard, and the clouds were low," Duet said. "I thought only ducks flew in that weather. But coming back from a hunt, running in my boat, I looked up and there was a helicopter. Through a speaker, Hall told me to stop, that he was a Fish and Wildlife Service agent."

Hall landed and checked Duet's license and birds, found him legal, then told Duet something he's never forgotten.

"'Jesse,' he said to me, 'look toward the gulf. See the miles and miles of freshwater marsh? In your lifetime, it'll be gone. It's disappearing faster than anyone thought. It'll all be saltwater in not too many years.'

"I said to him, 'Mr. Hall, you might know something about ducks. But you sure don't know anything about the marsh. It's been here since I was a kid. It'll be here long after I'm gone.'"

Nearly 20 years later, in 1988, Duet is 69 years old and still alive. But the freshwater marshes that once lay between his duck camp and the Gulf of Mexico have largely disappeared. In their place are vast expanses of salt and brackish water.

Hall was right.

"When I was young," Duet said, "my father trapped as many as 500

137

muskrats a day near my camp. Now there are very few muskrats around here. It was nothing for us to catch 1,000 bullfrogs in a couple of nights. Water moccasins were plentiful, too. The bullfrogs are gone. The water moccasins are gone. Saltwater, that's what's done it."

Gone too are thousands of ducks that once wintered near Jesse's camp. Dependent on freshwater vegetation, the ducks have relocated in search of water that is fresh, or, at worst, mildly brackish. Studies have shown that ducks much prefer freshwater marshes to saltwater or even brackish water.

Since before the nation was settled, millions of North American waterfowl have wintered in Louisiana's vast coastal marshes. Stretching approximately 250 miles from the Texas border to the Louisiana–Mississippi line, the marshes represent as much as 40 percent of all U.S. coastal wetlands. Each year, more than 50 percent of Mississippi Flyway and Central Flyway ducks winter in the marshes, as do hundreds of thousands of snow geese.

Other Central and Mississippi flyway ducks stop along the Louisiana coast en route to Mexico and points south.

Where the birds will go if Louisiana's marshes continue to disappear, or become unacceptably saline, nobody knows.

The birds' relocation is part of a Louisiana ecological disaster of massive proportions. How the situation evolves—or devolves—likely will affect everyone in Louisiana, and perhaps the nation.

Complicating the problem, at least for ducks, is the loss of thousands of acres of flooded timberland in northern Louisiana, Mississippi, and Arkansas.

All of it, say wildlife managers, portends bad times for ducks—and big challenges for duck managers.

"It's ominous," said Robert Stewart Jr., director of the National Wetlands Research Center in Slidell, Louisiana. The center is operated by the U.S. Fish and Wildlife Service. "Saline levels vary from area to area in the marsh, but it's becoming more saline in a hurry. As it does, emergent vegetation that ducks depend on for food disappears.

"We're losing to erosion up to 50 square miles of coastal marsh a year," Stewart said. "It's an unbelievable rate. If it continues, entire parishes [counties] will be gone in a relatively few years. The magnitude of the problem is beyond most people's imagination. To think we have lost half of that part of the active Mississippi delta formed since the year 1400, and that we lost it in 25 years! That's the size of the problem we're dealing with. It's amazing, really."

There are no easy solutions. Irrevocable decisions made by the state of Louisiana and by the Army Corps of Engineers preclude an immediate reversal.

Primary among causes of the problem has been the state's nearly willy-nilly issuance of permits to oil and gas exploration companies that allows them to build canals in the marshes. Since before World War II Louisiana's marshes have been a major U.S. supplier of oil and natural gas, and until the recent collapse of oil prices, no expense was spared by the industry in its quest for new supplies.

Because saltwater is heavier than freshwater, the former has used—and continues to use—canals built by the oil and gas companies (among other canals) to "intrude" on Louisiana's coastal marshes. The canals are thus accelerating to warp-speed a transition—from freshwater marsh to saltwater marsh—that otherwise would have occurred over many generations.

Complicating the problem, the Army Corps of Engineers, to prevent flooding and enhance river navigation, among other reasons, has in recent decades channelized and leveed the Mississippi, in effect "taming" its mouth. Once resembling a loose garden hose that annually sprayed its freshwater-laced, nutrient-rich mud in a thousand directions, the river now runs nearly straight to the gulf, carrying most of its freshwater and silt toward, and over, the continental shelf.

Without infusion of freshwater from the river, and without the Mississippi's nutrient-rich mud, the marshes, virtually defenseless against

139

the gulf's ever-pressing saltwater, are subsiding.

"People who live in the marshes, the Cajuns, they're seeing a way of life pass before them," Stewart said. "I've talked to Cajuns who can stand on a dock and for as far as they can see it's saltwater. These same people say it used to take two or three days in a pirogue to get through the marsh to saltwater."

John Trowbridge, Louisiana Universities Marine Consortium education officer, said people living throughout Louisiana will suffer as marshland degeneration continues.

"These estuarine areas, or marshes, are the nursery grounds for oysters, for crabs, for shrimp, and for several species of commercially important fish, such as red fish and trout," Trowbridge said. "At some time in their life cycle, each spends time in the freshwater marshes.

"Affected by the loss will be ducks, yes. But also affected will be Louisiana's fishing industry. In pounds produced, Louisiana is the largest seafood producer in the nation." Nearly half of the nation's fur is harvested from Louisiana's coastal marshes as well, according to some estimates.

The fact that sea levels worldwide have been rising in recent years is a complicating factor, Stewart said, but relatively speaking is not of major significance at this time. "It's what man has done that's caused the problem," he said.

Also affecting Mississippi Flyway ducks on their wintering grounds is the loss of bottomland hardwood forests. In its supplemental environmental impact statement filed before the 1987 waterfowl season, the Fish and Wildlife Service detailed the problem's scope.

"The bottomland hardwood forests of the lower Mississippi Floodplain are among the nation's most important wetlands," the report said. "They are prime overwintering grounds for many North American waterfowl, including 2.5 million of the 3 million mallards of the Mississippi Flyway, nearly all of the 4 million wood ducks, and many other migratory birds.

"Originally, the Mississippi Alluvial Plain included nearly 24 million acres of bottomland forested wetlands. By 1937, only 11.8 million acres, or 50 percent, of these remained. Today, there are fewer than 5.2 million acres left, roughly 20 percent of the original acreage.

"Over half of this wetland is in Louisiana, with large amounts also in Arkansas and Mississippi. These forested wetlands have been cleared and drained for crop production. Federal flood control projects and small watershed projects have accelerated wetland conversion to cropland, especially from the 1950s to the present.

"An estimated 2 percent of the remaining bottomland forests are lost annually."

Waterfowl researchers believe southern hardwood bottomlands—like southern coastal marshes—play important but as yet poorly understood roles in the life cycles of wintering ducks. The ducks use the disappearing marshes and bottomlands at different times, and perhaps for different purposes, the researchers theorize.

One purpose, especially for female birds, is to build strength for the spring breeding season. But as wintering grounds are lost or altered dramatically (from freshwater to brackish marsh, for example), a bird's ability to strengthen itself may also be diminished, the researchers say, thus reducing its chance to nest successfully upon return north.

"Ducks feed at different times on different things," Stewart said. "There is growing concern that food provided in the flooded hardwoods provides ducks, mallards in particular, with nutrition they need to successfully nest. It takes a lot of strength to nest, especially if, due to predation or other factors, a hen must nest twice or more in order to do so successfully.

"What we're thinking now is that a lack of quality wintering habitat may play a role in a duck's ability to nest successfully up north. Thus the wintering grounds become all the more important in the total picture."

Also of concern is the fact that ducks concentrate as habitat shrinks, thus making the birds easier prey for hunters. Perhaps more importantly, waterfowl concentration increases the chance some duck species will contract population-crippling diseases.

Traditionally, duck managers, both public and private, have stressed the importance of northern breeding grounds in maintaining waterfowl populations at maximum levels.

The reason is simple: Given sufficient water and habitat in the North, and a strong breeding population, ducks can quite literally be made each spring by the multiples of millions.

In recent years, however, as drought on the Canadian prairies has continued and as additional habitat has been lost to agriculture in the Dakotas, in Minnesota, and across Manitoba, Saskatchewan, and Alberta, the equation governing waterfowl production has grown astronomically more complex.

Consequently, everything affecting ducks has increased in importance. Hunting pressure. Illegal harvest. Predation. Wintering-ground quality. Once nearly overlooked by duck managers, each is now under close scrutiny.

Stewart, of the National Wetlands Research Center, said he is encouraged that momentum is shifting in the South, and that various federal agencies, together with the state of Louisiana, are ready to tackle head-on the problem of coastal erosion.

"We have some demonstration projects planned we hope can be eventually implemented to stop or at least slow the erosion of Louisiana's coastal wetlands," he said.

Louisiana's governor-elect, Buddy Roemer, also is eager to see the problem addressed and has appointed a blue-ribbon panel to propose solutions. The state's economic future, already precarious because of the decline of the oil and gas industries, is quite literally at stake.

142

Private conservation groups such as The Nature Conservancy and Ducks Unlimited are also taking increasingly active roles in the preservation of wildlife habitat in the South.

None of it can happen too soon for Jesse Duet.

"I never, ever thought I would live long enough to see what has happened down here," he said.

None of it can happen too soon for Bill Mellor, either.

Mellor, a Louisiana native and special agent of the U.S. Fish and Wildlife Service, is a pilot who frequently traverses Louisiana's coastal marshes, looking down from above at what he considers a vanishing American treasure.

"What I see is ducks disappearing," Mellor said. "What ducks remain are shifting around a lot. They're not in the same places they used to be. They're moving, trying to find the grasses and other food they need to survive.

"What I fear is that we get another strong hurricane like Juan, the one we had in 1985. Despite the erosion, we have a lot of good marsh left, more marsh, actually, than we have ducks. But a good hurricane could wipe out a lot of what we have.

"What the ducks need is someone to give them a break."

Mexico critical to ducks' future

SUNDAY, MARCH 27, 1988

Mexico City—North America's declining duck populations likely will push farther south in future winters, especially into Mexico, as habitat along the Gulf Coast of Louisiana and in the Central Valley of California—each of which now winters between a fifth and a quarter of the continent's ducks—continues to be lost.

More than 50 percent of Mississippi and Central flyway ducks winter in Louisiana, where hundreds of square miles of coastal marsh and bottomland hardwood habitat are lost or compromised annually.

In California, more than 70 percent of Pacific Flyway shoveler and gadwall populations and 80 percent of Pacific Flyway pintails winter in the Central Valley, where about 90 percent of the approximately 4 million acres of wetlands that existed before human settlement have been drained.

What awaits North America's ducks as they shift migration patterns and fly south of the border in future years is largely unknown, according to U.S. and Canadian waterfowl experts. There simply isn't enough research data available. This is especially true in Mexico, where an estimated 10 to 15 percent of North American ducks winter.

144

"Mexico will likely become very critical to waterfowl in the near future," said Art Brazda, a veteran U.S. Fish and Wildlife Service biologist and pilot who has flown waterfowl surveys in Mexico since 1962.

"Unfortunately, we know very little about what is going on down there and have little control over matters there that affect ducks and geese."

But what wildlife experts know isn't encouraging: Some waterfowl habitat is disappearing and there is virtually no enforcement of game laws. On the positive side, national conservation efforts are beginning, led by Ducks Unlimited of Mexico.

The Mexican Wildlife Service has little data upon which to gauge fluctuations in waterfowl populations or changes in habitat. Underfunded and understaffed, the service is plagued by frequent changes in leadership and a general lack of direction.

Moreover, in a country rife with social and financial problems, conservation of wildlife is a low priority. Which helps explain the Mexican Wildlife Service's ineffectiveness. Still, Mexican officials in recent weeks signed an agreement in Mexico City supplementing the North American Waterfowl Management Plan, a blueprint for waterfowl recovery previously agreed to by the United States and Canada.

Central to that recovery, of course, is waterfowl habitat. Some Mexican sloughs routinely run dry due to drought or water diversion for agriculture. Other marshes, especially those in the Central Highlands region, are drained by farmers; while some lakes and marshes south of Vera Cruz on Mexico's East Coast and west of Mexico City near Guadalajara are polluted by sewage, industrial and petroleum waste, and agrichemicals.

"The bad news is that in conservation and environmental regulation, Mexico is 40 or 50 years behind the U.S.," said Guy Baldassarre, assistant professor of wildlife science at the College of Environmental Science and Forestry at the State University of New York in Syracuse. Baldassarre oversees Mexican and American graduate students who study wildlife in Mexico. "The good news is that Mexico is also 50 years behind the U.S. and Canada in habitat loss. They still have a lot of good waterfowl habitat in Mexico."

But the hunting of waterfowl, particularly ducks, occurs with virtually no enforcement in Mexico. Nearly all hunting in Mexico is done by Americans, many of whom have recently experienced fewer opportunities to hunt in the United States due to declining waterfowl populations and increased costs associated with the lease or purchase of hunting land.

Most hunting in Mexico occurs along the Gulf Coast south of Brownsville, Texas; in the mangrove swamps on the Yucatan coast; in the Central Highlands; along the northern half of the West Coast; and in Baja California.

"There is virtually no data on the subject, but I think there is a growing fraternity of American hunters who go to Mexico to recapture what they used to have in the U.S. in terms of duck hunting," said Gary Kramer, refuge manager of the Salton Sea National Wildlife Refuge near Calipatria, California, and an expert on waterfowl and waterfowl hunting on the West Coast of Mexico.

Some hunting outfitters in Mexico suggest openly in advertisements that there is virtually no limit to the number of ducks a hunter can kill while in camp. The Mexican national daily duck limit that can be legally killed by a hunter is 15, more than three times the number that can be taken legally in many parts of the United States

"No matter how much we keep telling people that the ducks they're shooting in Mexico are the same ducks we have in the U.S. and Canada, they can't seem to get it through their thick heads," Brazda said.

Some outfitters not far from Culiacan near the West Coast, one of Mexico's prime waterfowl areas, have even petitioned the government to increase the daily limit to 20, and are optimistic they will succeed.

One camp visited near Culiacan had little need for increased limits. With few exceptions, hunters in the camp—all Americans—each day shot whatever number of ducks they were capable of shooting in the approximately four hours they were in the marsh.

One day, one hunter killed more than 80 ducks. The camp owner employs airboats to move birds over hunters' blinds.

Because no studies have been undertaken to determine hunter harvest in Mexico, the impact hunters in Mexico have on North American waterfowl can only be estimated.

"In the relative scheme of things—that is, considering the number of ducks killed each year in Canada and especially the U.S.—the number of birds taken by hunters in Mexico is probably not too significant," Kramer said. "For example, in one county in California, more than 300,000 ducks are killed annually by hunters. It could be that there aren't many more than that killed by hunters each year in all of Mexico."

Baldassarre agrees, but adds:

"It may be that the total bag taken by hunters in Mexico is, in the overall sense, not very significant. But composition of that bag could be very important, and for that reason I'd like to see studies undertaken to determine the numbers of each species taken by hunters.

"Pintails, especially, are in trouble now, and with the decline of habitat in California, where many Pacific Flyway pintails have traditionally wintered, it's likely more of them are now wintering in Mexico. If a major part of the bag taken there is found to be pintails, that could be very significant. As these populations decline, they might not be able to sustain too much pressure."

Rodrigo Migoya, a 30-year-old Auburn University graduate student, conducted a harvest survey during the recent four-month season at Patolandia, a duck-hunting camp near Culiacan. It is the first known such study to be conducted in Mexico.

"What I found was that in the four-month season, 10,500 ducks were killed at the camp by hunters," Migoya said. "The average number of hunters in the marsh each day over the period was 10, though the marsh wasn't hunted every day. The species composition was about 50 percent green-winged teal, 20 percent shovelers, 10 percent cinnamon teal, and 10 percent pintails."

In other camps nearby, Migoya said, pintails, not green-winged teal, may represent as much as 50 percent of the total bag.

147

Even if the total number of ducks killed by hunters doesn't significantly impact the continental waterfowl population, Brazda, of the Fish and Wildlife Service, and other experienced observers of waterfowl in Mexico worry that a tradition of high-kill hunting by Americans is intensifying in Mexico.

This situation may worsen, these observers believe, as hunting opportunities become fewer in the United States and as an increasing number of American hunters can afford to travel to Mexico.

The 60 percent decline—from 150 million to about 62 million—in the continental duck population in the past four decades, and the continuing loss of U.S. wintering habitat, heightens the Mexican hunting issue in importance, these waterfowl experts believe.

Ducks Unlimited of Mexico (DUMAC) appears to be the bright light of waterfowl conservation in Mexico. Though small—it has approximately 13,000 members—and only about 14 years old, the organization nevertheless may represent the best hope waterfowl have in Mexico.

"One of DUMAC's biggest advantages is that it has had the same leaders for a period of time and will continue to have the same leaders consistently," Baldassarre said. "They have undertaken some habitat projects, are distributing nest boxes to help tree ducks, are helping to educate Mexican students in wildlife management, and are helping to develop conservation concerns in the country. So they are doing some good, and will do more good in the future. DUMAC'S best years are ahead of it."

Like Ducks Unlimited Canada, DUMAC is not directly affiliated with Ducks Unlimited Inc., headquartered in suburban Chicago. There is a crossover of some board members of the three groups, and the organizations are bound in other manners, both direct and indirect. But they nevertheless retain separate leaders with separate focuses.

Still, Ducks Unlimited Inc. each year sends money to Ducks Unlimited Mexico. "This year, Ducks Unlimited Inc. has budgeted

$1,050,000 for DUMAC," said Ducks Unlimited Inc. executive vice president Matthew B. Connolly Jr. The money is used for habitat projects, conservation education, research station development, and general operations.

DUMAC's other funds are raised in much the same manner funds are raised in the United States by Ducks Unlimited Inc.—through corporate donations and by hosting fund-raising banquets.

Auburn student Migoya, who has worked for the Mexican Wildlife Service, agrees with Baldassarre that DUMAC and various Mexican universities, not the service, are Mexico's leaders in wildlife conservation.

"In the three years I worked with the wildlife service," Migoya said, "we had four different directors. Every time the top men changed, all the people in key positions changed, too. Routinely, people who don't know anything about biology or ecology get the important jobs. That's why it's left to conservation groups like DUMAC to take the lead."

Every three years, pilots of the U.S. Fish and Wildlife Service fly Mexico's East Coast, Central Highlands, and West Coast in an attempt to count ducks and geese.

This year, Brazda of Lafayette, Louisiana, and fellow pilots Doug Benning of Golden, Colorado, and Jim Voelzer of Portland, Oregon, conducted the surveys.

Brazda flew the East Coast (counting Mississippi and Central flyway ducks and geese), Benning flew the Central Highlands (Central Flyway), and Voelzer flew the West Coast (Pacific Flyway).

Of the three, Brazda, a North Dakota native and former Navy pilot, who also flies waterfowl surveys in Canada, is the most experienced.

"The purpose of the surveys is to assess the status of the habitat and determine the distribution of birds," said Brazda, who only recently flew his float-equipped Cessna 185 back to Lafayette, Louisiana, from the Yucatan.

"From what I have been able to observe, we don't have a signifi-

149

cant loss of habitat in Mexico yet. But the situation is extremely fragile. A lot of it can be lost in a period of two or three years. Agriculture takes some of it, and the old companies ruin some of it by dumping their waste in the marsh, though this situation is improving. And the political system in Mexico is such that there is not a lot of emphasis on wildlife or wildlife habitat.

"You have to remember that in Mexico, the middle class—which in any society accounts for most major changes that occur—is almost totally lacking. In Mexico, either you've got it or you don't, there's not much middle ground. And the guy who lives in the shack in Mexico has other things to worry about than politics, namely feeding his family. Consequently, because he doesn't worry much about politics, he doesn't worry much about his environment, either."

Brazda, who found overall East Coast duck numbers down 6 percent from 1982, his most recent comparable survey (pintails were down 41 percent, gadwalls down 21 percent, wigeon down 62 percent—all offset by green-winged teal, which were up 122 percent and blue-winged teal, up 61 percent), believes American hunters have an impact on waterfowl, particularly ducks, that winter in Mexico.

"Unless there's a change in Mexico in hunting regulations, Americans will present a great and real threat to wintering ducks. I think the gringo who goes to Mexico and kills 200 ducks is having just as big an impact on the resource as if he killed them in North Dakota.

"Any gringo who goes to Mexico just to kill, kill, kill—I'll tell you what, there's something wrong with that bastard's mind.

"The bottom line is this: Anytime you take a resource that we're only half-ass managing and you subject it to a severe loss of habitat and constant hunting pressure, you can't help but have a disastrous result, no matter where the killing is taking place."

Gary Kramer, the manager of Salton Sea refuge in California who is an experienced hunter of ducks in Mexico, shares Brazda's concern but believes the problem of American hunters overharvesting ducks in

Mexico is self-limiting.

"One reason is that there are a certain number of American duck hunters who wouldn't step in Mexico for all the money in the world, to hunt or to do anything else," Kramer said. "Also, keep in mind that for the most part, Mexicans don't hunt ducks, so that removes a large number of potential hunters from the picture. And, in my opinion, there are only so many camps that can be set up in Mexico to accommodate Americans."

The only way to fly from Culiacan to Mazatlan on the West Coast is to charter an airplane; there is no scheduled service.

If you make the flight in February, leaving Culiacan by 9:00 A.M., the temperature will be near 80 degrees Fahrenheit, with a cloudless sky overhead. Similar weather will greet you in Mazatlan.

En route, stretching below as far as the eye can see, are miles and miles and miles of vegetable fields, tomatoes mostly, with bunches of workers bent over the plants pruning, hoeing and, in general, caring for the multi-million dollar crops.

"All of those vegetables are headed for the States," the pilot says. "You can see up in the mountains where the streams have been dammed and water diverted into the fields. That's how the crops are irrigated."

It is this change of land use that U.S. Fish and Wildlife Service pilots Benning and Voelzer saw when they flew waterfowl surveys over Mexico this year.

Voelzer found ducks on the West Coast down 38 percent from 1985 and down 50 percent from 1982, with green-winged teal (down 69 percent from 1982), blue-winged teal (down 39 percent) and pintails (down 51 percent) all off by significant margins.

In the Central Highlands, on the other hand, Benning surveyed ducks that, overall, were up 59 percent over 1985, with green-winged teal higher by 43 percent. Shovelers, meanwhile, were down 24 percent, and canvasbacks down 13 percent.

Brazda, Voelzer, and Benning have sent their survey results to U.S. Fish and Wildlife Service headquarters in Washington, D.C., where they will be analyzed and compared to mid-winter waterfowl surveys conducted in the United States, and compared as well to long-term wintering duck population averages.

"Overall, I think things are getting a little better in Mexico regarding wildlife," said Rodrigo Migoya, the Auburn student. "I think there's an increase in the number of people taking an interest in wildlife. It's a small increase, perhaps. But it's an increase. The big thing is there just isn't much information available about the subject, and there isn't much money available to get it."

Hunters in Mexico riddle duck limits

MONDAY, MARCH 28, 1988

Culiacan, Mexico—Jose "Pity" Salomon sits in the shade of the open-air structure that is his duck camp headquarters, looks out over his huge marsh, and says, "All of this is new habitat."

Indeed it is. Stretching five miles wide by 20 miles long, the marsh is the result of water being dammed in the distant mountains and diverted for irrigation of crops.

The newly channelized water was directed through thousands of acres of vegetable fields beginning about 15 years ago. Then, heavily laden with fertilizers, it spilled into the freshwater lagoon that Salomon's duck hunters—nearly all American—now ply in airboats four months a year, November through February.

The fertilized water quite literally "grew" a marsh. With it came waterfowl and other birds, some of them pushed into western Mexico by a loss of wintering habitat in California.

"Most people living here would not have been able to see what was happening to my marsh," says Salomon. "But because I am a pilot who owns a charter aircraft company, I could see when I flew over it something new was occurring below; that new plant life was forming and that ducks were starting to stay in the marsh."

A successful businessman and duck hunter, Salomon saw an opportunity and, thinking he could capture a piece of the growing Ameri-

153

can duck-hunter trade, leased the marsh from the government and built his camp.

Seven years later, in 1988, Salomon is enjoying the fruits of his efforts. His camp is frequented each day of the season by American hunters who oftentimes, for a three-day trip, pay in excess of $2,000, including air fare, for warm weather and ducks.

Salomon delivers plenty of both.

At Patolandia ("Duckland," the name given Salomon's camp), 10,500 ducks were killed in the 1987–1988 season, nearly all of them by Americans, a majority of whom, it is estimated, shot in excess of their legal limit of 15 birds daily while in camp.

Virtually all of the ducks were migrants from the United States and Canada, where limits of from three to five birds per day are common.

Rodrigo Migoya, a Mexican and an Auburn University graduate student, lived at Salomon's camp throughout the hunting season and conducted a waterfowl harvest survey, the first of its kind in Mexico.

In addition to counting the number of ducks that hunters killed, Migoya aged the birds, sexed them, weighed them, and checked their feeding habits.

He also observed hunters in camp.

"From what I was able to determine, about 30 percent came to Mexico to hunt ducks just for the adventure," Migoya said. "They were not overly capable as hunters, and in the four hours a day hunters typically spent in the marsh, they were not capable of killing much in excess of their 15-bird daily limit, if they reached that.

"Another 15 percent of hunters were conscientious. They were capable of killing many birds, but restricted themselves either to the legal limit or to less than that by selectively shooting only drakes or certain species.

"The other 55 percent were both capable of shooting many ducks in excess of their limits and willing to do it. The most one hunter took this year in his four hours in the marsh was about 80. Others took 50, 60, whatever."

In Mexico, especially among duck-camp outfitters, Pity Salomon, an intelligent, creative man, is known as a conservationist. He has worked hard to develop his marsh, is a strong supporter of DUMAC—Ducks Unlimited of Mexico—and has developed a strategy to "rest" his marsh at certain times to benefit the many thousands of birds that winter there.

Still, Salomon in many instances allows American hunters to shoot whatever number of ducks they want, an enterprise facilitated by the use of airboats, which are employed by camp workers to "herd" ducks over hunters' blinds.

Among other explanations for allowing hunters to overshoot their limits, Salomon reasons that, even with excessive individual shooting, Mexico accounts for only a small fraction of the total number of birds hunters kill each year in the United States and Canada. In that respect, he is correct.

"I prefer to offer quality hunts," Salomon says. "But I don't want to scare the ducks out of my marsh by overshooting it. That's why I rest it regularly.

"Through our outfitter association, we try to police our ranks by keeping a list of American hunters who are abusive in the number of ducks they want to shoot. There are some who get angry if you ask them to restrict the numbers of ducks they kill. The names of these people we try to circulate to all outfitters, so they don't book them into camp again. Business is good. We don't need that type of person in camp."

That fact notwithstanding, according to Mexicans familiar with the duck-hunting business south of the U.S. border, it is competition among outfitters that has helped foster excessive kills by American hunters.

"Camp owners fear that if they restrict hunters to legal limits, they will lose business to other camps that don't restrict them," said Eric W. Gustafson, executive vice president of DUMAC, headquartered in the city of Monterrey, Mexico. "To stop this, we have to get the association

155

of outfitters to, in unison, agree to restrict hunters to the legal limit. Then they won't have to worry about losing any clients to other outfitters. DUMAC is working toward that end."

The question then becomes, would American duck hunters, already accustomed to big kills in Mexico and suffering in recent years from restricted bag limits and hunting opportunity in the United States, be willing to pay thousands of dollars for a legal Mexican hunt?

Some might. Others wouldn't.

"I'm not sure how many Americans would pay a significant sum of money to come down here to shoot a limited number of birds," said Mike Dick, a Large, Pennsylvania, businessman who in February hunted at Patolandia with his wife.

Jim Bohrer of Germantown, Maryland, was in Salomon's camp with the Pennsylvania couple.

"Obviously, people go to Mexico because there is a great profusion of birds," Bohrer said. "I'm not sure anyone would go to Mexico to hunt if they had the same limits we have in the U.S. Among reasons for this is the fact that warm-weather duck hunting is not duck hunting as most Americans appreciate it. You're not hunting with your dog or your decoys. It's all unfamiliar stuff.

"But if you like to gun, Mexico can be an exquisite trip. You experience a tremendous amount of gunning in a very short period of time. The way it's done with the airboats is exciting and fun, but it's a lot less sporting than, say, hunting on the Eastern Shore of Maryland, where I usually hunt. Actually, the Mexican hunt is a lot more shooting than hunting. The real sportsman might tire of it if he did it more than a couple times a year.

"As for shooting so many birds and how I feel about it, that's a complex question. I guess I feel people with resources will always find a way to get to where ducks are and find a way to kill them. But I also believe people who kill ducks also spend a lot of money and time helping to preserve ducks. I, for instance, try to replace what I take in mul-

156

tiples, and not only so I can shoot them. I just enjoy just seeing them.

"But overall, in my opinion, the harvesting of ducks is just a minor part of the problem of declining duck populations. The bigger issue is the loss of wetlands and marshes on the breeding grounds up north."

Pity Salomon offers a pair of ear protectors to a visitor, dons a pair himself, and cranks over the engine on his airboat. The engine sputters, catches, and spins the boat's huge propeller, moving the craft away from shore and into the marsh.

Salomon's mission: to show his marsh to the visitor and to check his hunters.

En route there is no talking. Even with ear protectors, the boat's engine is excessively loud. Too, airboats are unforgiving to careless operators, so there is little time for conversation.

As Salomon increases the craft's speed, the marsh flies by, the warm air pressing against the visitor's face, ducks skittering along the shallow water's surface in attempts to avoid the oncoming boat.

When he reaches open water, Salomon stops the engine and talks into a microphone attached to his ear protectors. Each of Salomon's seven airboats is wired in this manner for sound, enabling drivers to communicate not only with other drivers, but with bird boys assigned to hunters' blinds, each of whom carries a portable two-way radio.

When joined by two other airboats, Salomon accelerates and the boats fan out, their operators communicating with one another by radio, heading in the general direction of a hunter's blind, located perhaps a mile distant. One boat goes left, another right. Salomon stays in the center, jogging back and forth, seeking out ducks, finding them and forcing them into the air toward the blind.

Airboats are necessary for this type of shooting because without them ducks wouldn't fly with any consistency, and a hunter's chance of taking significant numbers of birds would be drastically reduced. Mexico is a land blessed with warm weather and calm winds, and under such

157

conditions ducks don't often do anything but swim and eat.

As the boats near the blind, they close ranks, literally herding a few hundred ducks toward the hunter. Above the engine noise, the sound of a shotgun report can be heard, and from the blind a bird boy emerges, his bare feet buried in mud as he retrieves a downed green-winged teal, pintail, or shoveler—the most prevalent duck species in Salomon's marsh.

This time, in this drive, the hunter—a Mexican friend of Salomon's—bags only a few birds. Most of the ducks fly past him out of range, others are missed due to poor marksmanship.

Salomon pulls up to the blind, kills the engine, and engages in playful banter with his friend. The day is beautiful, the marsh flush with ducks, and, back at camp, the cook is preparing a meal of duck, dove, shrimp, and beer.

"Let's eat," Salomon says.

Zane Markowitz of Reston, Virginia, traveled to Patolandia with his friend Jim Bohrer. It is one of many trips the two have taken together to hunt, some of the sojourns ending at destinations as distant as Scotland, where they shoot upland birds both driven and walked-up.

"Why go to Mexico?" Markowitz asks rhetorically. "To extend the season, I guess. I don't get to hunt a lot during the year, so this provides another opportunity. Plus, we'd never been to Mexico before, and we'd heard for so many years about the huge concentrations of birds and how fabulous the hunting is.

"Pity runs a great camp and is a gracious host, and that helps make a trip fun. The hunting was fun, too. The airboats aren't as active or as obtrusive as you might think they would be, so that's a plus. And there are plenty of birds."

Like Bohrer and most other capable duck hunters who visit Mexico, Markowitz killed significantly more than his legal limit while in camp.

Asked why, he says:

"I don't know. I've never thought about it. I wouldn't do it at home,

I know that. Duck numbers have fallen off so much along the Eastern Shore, I don't know what can be done to bring them back to what they once were.

"I know I work hard individually to do what I can to help ducks, and not just because I want to shoot them. I think ducks and duck hunting represent a major part of our North American heritage, and I'd hate to see it lost.

"But would I have had as much fun if I had killed just the 15-bird limit instead of what I did kill? Yes, I would have. I don't really know why I didn't stop at 15. It's a good question, but difficult to answer.

"A lot of emotions go into it. Maybe it's just that some people have more hunt in them than others."

Mexican
duck advocates
take bold steps

TUESDAY, MARCH 29, 1988

Mazatlan, Mexico—A billboard on the outskirts of this resort town offers an unusual greeting for vacationers. The sign is not that of a hotel, restaurant, or rental car company. Instead, it features DUMAC—Ducks Unlimited of Mexico—and suggests interested parties join the organization to help preserve waterfowl habitat in Mexico.

In a country whose masses are poor and in which a broad-based conservation ethic is virtually non-existent, DUMAC represents a bold initiative. With only 13,000 members and a total annual budget of but $1.3 million—about $1 million coming from Ducks Unlimited Inc. in suburban Chicago—DUMAC is attempting to preserve habitat in Mexico while raising the consciousness of Mexicans about the many benefits of wildlife.

Whether DUMAC, now in its 14th year, can save habitat and educate people faster than habitat is destroyed and faster than the burgeoning human population in Mexico expands is anyone's guess. Intensified agricultural practices must also be countered before they continue to ruin North American waterfowl wintering habitat.

An estimated 10 to 15 percent of the continent's ducks now winter in Mexico. Experts believe that percentage may increase markedly in the near future, as southern U.S. habitat traditionally used by ducks continues to be lost or compromised.

Eric Gustafson, the Mexican executive director of DUMAC, thinks his organization will succeed in its mission. DUMAC is headquartered in the northern industrial city of Monterrey.

"We're trying hard," Gustafson said. "It's a difficult situation in Mexico, considerably different than dealing with conservation in the U.S. and Canada. In my opinion, our probability of holding off Mexico's other conservation problems is very, very high. Our work is exponential in the way it affects others. We employ people, we rebuild habitat. Things are going very well, considering the conditions under which we work."

Such conditions include the fact that to accomplish anything on the Mexican conservation front, a massive and oftentimes grossly inefficient government bureaucracy must be overcome. Rather than dealing with one federal agency, for instance, Gustafson and his colleagues frequently must concern themselves with three, each of which governs its own turf.

Example: To fly aerial surveys that count ducks and geese and assess habitat, the U.S. Fish and Wildlife Service must secure permits from the Mexican government.

But even this minor hurdle often poses problems for U.S. wildlife officials, and sometimes DUMAC officials are called upon to smooth the way with officials in Mexico City. Recently, in fact, DUMAC negotiated permits covering a 10-year span.

"You have to understand," Gustafson said, "DUMAC is different from Ducks Unlimited Inc. and Ducks Unlimited Canada. We concentrate on waterfowl, but we are a broader-based conservation organization than that. We work to benefit a number of different species, including deer, jaguar, white-winged dove, and quail.

"It's been said that in a poor country such as Mexico, conservation is a luxury, but it's also a dire necessity. Mexico has more than 1,000 birds, which is 50 percent more than the U.S. and Canada have combined. Because of this, and because there are so few conservation efforts underway in Mexico, we have taken on a broader spectrum than just

161

ducks, though they remain our main objective."

Gustafson, who holds a doctorate from the University of Massachusetts, joined DUMAC in 1982, eight years after it was founded. When hired, he found the organization stagnant, he said, with only three habitat projects completed from the organization's inception in 1974.

"One of the first things I did was reorganize DUMAC," Gustafson said. "We got good people on board and put our noses to the grindstone. We just dedicated our 70th project March 11 near Mazatlan. We have either developed or are now managing 654,000 acres of wildlife habitat."

In a year, DUMAC raises about $250,000 in Mexico, primarily by holding fund-raising dinners. Membership in the organization costs 20,000 pesos (about $8). Membership in Ducks Unlimited Inc., on the other hand, which raises in excess of $50 million a year, mainly in the United States, costs $20.

Among residents of the Twin Cities who are supporters of DUMAC are wildlife sculptor Bob Winship of North Oaks, who was DUMAC's first life sponsor, and Minneapolis auto dealer Win Stephens, also a life sponsor.

The amount DUMAC can grow in membership in Mexico is limited to some extent because so few Mexicans hunt ducks, according to Gustafson. In fact, according to some who are familiar with the organization, Mexicans who belong to DUMAC represent some of the wealthiest hunters in the nation.

"Duck hunting is too expensive for the average person in Mexico," Gustafson said. "Most Mexicans who hunt would rather go after something with some meat on it, such as a deer."

Though it raises considerably less money than Ducks Unlimited Inc., DUMAC can complete its projects considerably more cheaply than similar projects can be completed in the United States or Canada, thanks to inexpensive labor and materials.

"We can get five to six times the amount of acreage for our dollar,"

162

Gustafson said.

The average DUMAC project costs between $30,000 and $50,000 to complete. The amount of habitat that can be developed in Mexico for that amount of money differs substantially, depending on whether the project is in the arid north or, say, in the Yucatan, where water is more readily available.

The establishment and continued funding of waterfowl research centers in Mexico to be used by Mexican and American graduate students is also a DUMAC priority. A considerable amount of basic waterfowl research—accomplished long ago on birds in Canada and the United States—has yet to be undertaken in Mexico.

Until this research is done, waterfowl managers will have difficulty determining, for example, the nutritional requirements of ducks wintering in Mexico.

All of which poses a massive challenge to a relatively small organization.

Dial Dunkin, an American living in Harlingen, Texas, who guides bird hunters in Mexico, believes the challenge may be too big.

"If you were God, and you wanted to do something for ducks in Mexico, what would you do?" Dunkin asked. "It's a big country, with poor people and a lot of problems. Accomplishing something there to benefit wildlife will be very, very difficult."

Gustafson acknowledges the size of problems DUMAC faces—one of which is the theft of the organization's tree-duck boxes by Mexicans who want the materials for other uses—but thinks DUMAC projects that benefit people as well as wildlife will be appreciated in Mexico, and will help nurture in Mexicans a conservation ethic.

"Among species we benefit with our projects is man," Gustafson said. "Many of our projects are very labor intensive, and we hire a lot of people. That's good for everyone, because it helps them buy into our projects.

"Also, by creating a water resource, we not only get water for ducks,

163

the people get water for drinking, for their cattle, and for irrigation. All we ask is that enough water is kept in the project to support waterfowl. So giving to DUMAC benefits species other than ducks."

U.S. Wildlife Service will bolster forces to halt slaughter of ducks

APRIL 3, 1988

The director of the U.S. Fish and Wildlife Service will increase substantially the number of agents in waterfowl wintering grounds and will personally scrutinize this year's hunting regulations before they are completed.

Conceding the federal government has largely ignored U.S. waterfowl wintering grounds, Fish and Wildlife Service director Frank Dunkle is assigning five additional special agents to the Gulf Coast to protect ducks, geese, and other wildlife. Dunkle said he also will send a major portion of a 25-member graduating class of agent-trainees to that area in August.

The changes come in the wake of a series of articles published by the *Pioneer Press* in February that detailed widespread abuses of waterfowl laws in Louisiana, where state and federal agents—seven U.S. agents are permanently assigned to Louisiana—estimate the number of illegal ducks killed annually is four times the number killed legally.

"For too long we've said the problem facing waterfowl in North America was just a loss of habitat," Dunkle said. "It's not just habitat, it's everything. Hunting. Illegal hunting. Contaminants. Habitat loss. All of it affects our waterfowl populations."

Dunkle made his comments during an interview in the Twin Cities.

165

Dunkle also plans to intensify waterfowl enforcement in Louisiana, Arkansas, Texas, and Mississippi, as well as other states, by improving training for state and federal agents on temporary assignment in the South during waterfowl seasons.

Dunkle has ordered his information and education staff to produce videos and other material about waterfowl hunting ethics. He said he will examine U.S. waterfowl hunting regulations before they are completed by his agency late this summer. Dunkle said he will pay particular attention to season lengths, bag limits, and special seasons.

He also said he supports increased penalties for violators of waterfowl laws.

The *Pioneer Press* and the Izaak Walton League, along with other conservation groups in Minnesota and elsewhere, have organized a drive to buy a helicopter for federal agents in Louisiana, who say it will help reduce duck baiting.

Baiting allows illegal hunters to kill large numbers of birds by attracting them to corn, milo, or other feed placed near hunters' blinds.

One reformed Louisiana poacher, Ace Cullum of Monroe, a professional duck-hunting guide for more than 20 years, was in the Twin Cities at the Northwest Sportshow last weekend. He estimates the illegal kill in Louisiana is as high as 10 times the legal kill.

"For as long as anyone can remember, people in Louisiana have shot whatever number of ducks they wanted to shoot," Cullum said, adding that armed guards with two-way radios were assigned to protect hunters from agents at one club he operated. "A lot of us know now this was wrong and that it has hurt ducks. We're trying to get the situation cleaned up."

Dunkle, 63, former chief of the Montana Fish, Wildlife, and Parks Department, is regarded both inside and outside the service as a director who cares about waterfowl. In his two years in office, he has attempted to reorder the agency's priorities, emphasize enforcement of game laws—particularly laws prohibiting waterfowl baiting—and better equip

166

field managers and agents.

"I came to Washington because I thought I could help make this agency more effective, and because I thought its priorities were out of line," he said. "I'm not saying the things the service was doing weren't right. It's just that, through treaties and other mandates, the Congress has told us that waterfowl were one of our most important resources. We should manage them with that in mind."

As part of this effort, Dunkle said, federal and state agents assigned to Louisiana and other southern states during this fall's waterfowl season will attend orientation sessions to better acquaint themselves with the area. Federal agents assigned permanently to Louisiana have said the temporary agents could be more useful if they knew the terrain.

Under Dunkle, the Fish and Wildlife Service has developed and implemented the North American Waterfowl Management Program, an ambitious effort to secure and restore millions of acres of waterfowl habitat in the United States and Canada.

Total cost of the program will be about $1.5 billion, with funds coming from state, provincial, and federal governments of the United States and Canada, as well as from private conservation groups.

Ducks Unlimited makes hard choices

JUNE 12, 1988

Long Grove, IL—With North America's duck populations in severe decline, officials of Ducks Unlimited, the world's foremost waterfowl conservation organization, are planning major steps to alter the group's course.

Though Ducks Unlimited has raised and spent about $450 million restoring or protecting 5.1 million acres of U.S., Canadian, and Mexican wetlands, North American duck populations have nosedived by about 60 percent in the last four decades, from an estimated 150 million in the 1940s to about 60 million last year.

Due in large part to an extended drought now plaguing the U.S. and Canadian prairies, the continent's duck population may fall even lower this year, perhaps to 55 million, a number unprecedented in modern times. Habitat loss, pesticide use, and hunting have contributed to the decline.

Newly appointed Ducks Unlimited executive vice president Matthew B. Connolly Jr., widely respected in the conservation community, said he believes his reorganized staff is capable of leading the fight to return the continental population of ducks to 100 million.

168

In a major departure from his predecessor's directives on the subject, he also said Ducks Unlimited members are being told to expect cutbacks in season lengths and bag limits this fall, and that, in the future, if errors are to be made in these issues, "They should be made on the side of the ducks," without "quibbling and carping."

Historically, Ducks Unlimited leaders have pushed for longer seasons and bigger bag limits.

Connolly represents fresh leadership in Ducks Unlimited.

But sources within the organization say an entrenched, cumbersome volunteer hierarchy will make change difficult for the 550,000-member international organization headquartered in the Chicago suburb of Long Grove.

Sixty-one members serve on the Ducks Unlimited executive committee and 260 on its board.

Indeed, the group's history of politicking for greater opportunities for hunters makes a significant portion of its membership unfamiliar, if not uncomfortable, with restrictive hunting regulations. Some waterfowl managers believe such restrictions are needed during a time when ducks are being assaulted on nearly every front.

"I think hunter harvest is important, probably even critical, especially during this time of drought on the breeding grounds," said Bruce Batt, director of the Delta Waterfowl Research Center in Delta, Manitoba.

A four-month examination of Ducks Unlimited by the St. Paul *Pioneer Press* has found that—despite the multitude of good it has done for ducks and other wildlife—nearly from its inception in the 1930s it has attempted to mitigate waterfowl hunting regulations in the United States.

The non-political status the group claims in its original articles of incorporation dated January 29, 1937, is in conflict with these actions.

In fact, while Ducks Unlimited has repeatedly declined to take stands on environmental and resource issues adversely affecting ducks in the United States and Canada, such as the Cache River project in Arkansas and the Garrison Diversion project in North Dakota, it has nevertheless often intervened in the waterfowl-hunting regulatory process, most times seeking to liberalize hunting restrictions.

Such interventions range from buying drinks for state and federal waterfowl managers at annual flyway meetings, to correspondence of the kind recently obtained from the Department of the Interior through the Freedom of Information Act.

Dated July 25, 1969, a letter from past Ducks Unlimited President Henry G. Schmidt of Cleveland (Ducks Unlimited president 1965–1966) to then Assistant Secretary of the Interior Leslie Glasgow underscores the kind of influence-peddling Ducks Unlimited's leaders have practiced.

"I understand that Mr. Kenneth E. Crawford of the League of Ohio Sportsmen has made a request to appear before the National Waterfowl Advisory Committee. . . .," Schmidt wrote.

"Mr. Crawford has been very active in waterfowl affairs in this state and is also influential in Republican politics in the area. Although the latter has nothing to do with waterfowl, he is very sympathetic to the Nixon Administration and will do everything possible to be helpful in furthering the administration's interests, your interests and the general overall future of waterfowl. I trust you will accord him the privilege of appearing before the committee."

The newspaper has also learned that despite its repeated claims of being non-political, an examination of tax returns filed by Ducks Unlimited with the Internal Revenue Service shows it provided about $250,000 annually in recent years to the Wildlife Conservation Fund of America, an Ohio-based organization whose job for Ducks Unlimited has been to lobby in Washington, D.C., and elsewhere to counter attempts by anti-hunting groups to close federal refuges and other areas to hunting; that even though the organization's IRS exemption from federal income taxes defines Ducks Unlimited as, in large part, educational, it was only recently that Ducks Unlimited included in its statement of purpose an intention to "educate the general public concerning wetlands and waterfowl management"; that Ducks Unlimited has not used its magazine or other media to a significant extent to inform its adult members about legal behavior while hunting. Some observers believe the group's relative silence on this issue has helped foster the dismal image much of the group's hunting membership has in some areas of the country among game-law enforcement agents, and perhaps has also helped contribute to excessive illegal harvest in areas where ducks congregate.

"My quarrel with DU chiefly is that they never have been willing to put the hammer down on their members," said retired U.S. Fish and Wildlife Service agent-in-charge Willy J. Parker of Henderson, Kentucky, who oversaw migratory game law enforcement in the Chesapeake Bay region of Maryland and Virginia.

Parker is a life Ducks Unlimited sponsor.

"I have never seen any effort by DU leaders to encourage the membership to obey game laws." Parker said. "I think at least in part this is why we've busted so many of their members over the years, including some of their leaders. Most of the ones we caught were hunting either over bait or shooting over their limits.

"Invariably, almost to a person, when we caught them they'd say, 'Hey, I gave this or that or $10,000—or whatever—to Ducks Unlimited, so I guess maybe I deserve a few extra ducks.'

"I just can't understand that. Either you're a conservationist or you're not. A conservationist doesn't contribute money so he can take more."

Still, judged by money raised or habitat restored, Ducks Unlimited is a unique and, in many ways, wildly successful venture whose intensely loyal membership contributes—in addition to millions of dollars—countless volunteer hours.

And whatever the organization's shortcomings, Ducks Unlimited, together with other waterfowl and conservation groups and waterfowl hunters, has greatly improved the continent's resources through its work on behalf of ducks.

Founded during the Dust Bowl days of the 1930s, Ducks Unlimited was and largely remains an organization of waterfowl hunters, though the percentage of members who hunt has dropped from a one-time high of about 90 to a present low of 62.

Almost from the outset, Ducks Unlimited Inc., headquartered originally in New York City, was joined in its efforts by Ducks Unlimited Canada. The idea was that Ducks Unlimited Inc. would raise money in the United States to be sent to Ducks Unlimited Canada, which would do the actual hands-on habitat development. Reasoning that about 70 percent of North America's ducks are reared in Canada, the group's leaders believed this was the best use of available funds.

Thus was born Ducks Unlimited's "singleness of purpose" philosophy. Simply put, the organization's leaders said Ducks Unlimited's only intent in the United States was to raise money, and its only intent in Canada was to develop waterfowl habitat to improve duck populations.

By the late 1940s, Ducks Unlimited was raising about $400,000 a year and successfully completing Canadian projects, 40 of which were developed in 1949 alone.

But even then the group had its critics, including Aldo Leopold, considered by many to be the father of modern conservation. According to a recently released biography of Leopold published by the University of Wisconsin Press, Leopold believed Ducks Unlimited officials exaggerated by a wide margin what benefit their work actually had to North America's ducks.

Such criticism remains in some circles today. Some Ducks Unlimited national trustees have been led to believe the organization's impact on the continent's duck population is larger than it actually is. Usually, only about 3 percent to 5 percent of all duck production occurs on water and associated uplands controlled by Ducks Unlimited, according to Connolly.

172

"When I was a DU national trustee, I was told by other trustees and directors of the Ducks Unlimited staff that 75 percent or more of ducks that come down the Mississippi Flyway were ducks hatched on DU projects," said Jesse Fontenot, 67, of Morgan City, Louisiana, a former national Ducks Unlimited trustee. "At the time, I believed that, and I got up in front of a lot of people when I started Ducks Unlimited chapters in Louisiana and told those people that, and it was on that basis that many of them joined the organization.

"But I believe in finding out facts for myself. So I went to Canada on numerous occasions to look at DU projects and the situation in general, and I could see that this was not the case. When I confronted the DU people about this they told me just to look at the good, not the bad that the organization did.

"But I couldn't do that. I've always been a straight shooter and I've always told it the way it is. I couldn't get up in front of people and tell them one thing, and ask them to start a DU chapter, when I knew it wasn't true. It was in 1978 when I quit the organization."

Dan Baassen, of Wayzata, Minnesota, a member of Ducks Unlimited's executive committee, says no exaggeration is necessary to sell Ducks Unlimited in Minnesota or Wisconsin.

"We don't have to oversell up here," Baassen said. "People join DU in this part of the country because they believe, as I believe, that DU represents the future of waterfowl on this continent, and it's for that reason that they give of their time and money."

That members' time and money doesn't buy more than approximately 5 percent of the continent's annual duck production is not necessarily indicative of inefficiency on the part of Ducks Unlimited, Baassen said. Rather, it is telling, simply, of just how big the continent is.

Adds Connolly, the Ducks Unlimited executive vice president:

"That what we're doing isn't in and of itself enough to save ducks don't necessarily mean we shouldn't be doing it. What it means is that we have to do more. State, provincial, and federal governments have to do more. Other groups have to do more. Everyone has to do more."

Steady, if unspectacular, growth for Ducks Unlimited continued

through the 1950s and early 1960s. In 1965, Dale Whitesell of Colum-
bus, Ohio, was appointed executive vice president, and he, perhaps more
than anyone else in the organization, is responsible for the Ducks Unlimited that exists today—the good as well as the not-so-good.

Whatever else Whitesell will be remembered for, he will be im-
mortalized for developing the membership banquet into the money-
making tool it is today for Ducks Unlimited and a host of other local,
regional, and national conservation groups who have copied the idea.

In its simplest form, a Ducks Unlimited membership banquet involves selling tickets to a few hundred duck lovers, putting them in a big
hall, and raffling and auctioning duck-hunting and duck-related items.
Most towns of any size in Minnesota have such events annually.

In the year after Whitesell's appointment, Ducks Unlimited passed
the $1 million mark in funds raised. Growth continued incrementally.
By 1977, more than $13 million was raised in a 12-month period.

Not until last year, when Ducks Unlimited membership declined
in every state except Wisconsin, did growth stall (due to a membership-
cost hike, Connolly says, from $10 annually to $20). Even then, the
money continued to roll in. Nearly $60 million, a record, was raised in
1987.

The upside to the growth was that Ducks Unlimited was able to
undertake more projects in Canada, as well as the United States, than
ever before. The downside was that in this period of rapid growth, Ducks
Unlimited leaders let slide certain aspects of the organization that today's
leaders say they hope to address.

"Essentially, we 'grew up' in about a 10-year period," said Harry
Knight of Williamsburg, Virginia, who was recently elected president at
the group's Nashville convention. "We went from a very small organization to a very big organization in a very short time. As with any company undergoing rapid growth, there's a certain amount of fallout, a certain amount that doesn't get done.

"Education about hunting ethics and behavior is one example. If

174

you look back through our magazines, and in our [youth] Greenwings program, you'll see that we've had subtle messages at least occasionally about these issues.

"But we never have done much about it, and I think this is something that can be improved on a great deal. You have to remember, all of the early Ducks Unlimited leaders were avid hunters. And I think they felt they had to concern themselves with hunting regulations because they felt other people or groups were doing the same thing, but they were coming at it from the anti-hunting side.

"So maybe their responses, while well-intended, were too defensive. I don't necessarily apologize for what we've done, because we've done more for ducks than anyone else. But there are probably a lot of human sides to this equation that are understandable, given the circumstances of history."

Though almost no one in the organization will discuss the subject for the record, virtually everyone familiar with Ducks Unlimited's history agrees that Whitesell, who oversaw Ducks Unlimited's fast-growth period, was a gung-ho, no-nonsense leader who saw things one way—his way—and relegated other opinions, even those of some trustees and executive committee members, to the back burner.

Believing nesting habitat availability was virtually the only factor that affected duck populations, Whitesell, while executive director, stressed that hunting had no effect on waterfowl.

"You can't stockpile ducks," Whitesell would say, meaning that hunting or no hunting, duck populations would remain about constant, subject only to weather and habitat availability.

When the U.S. Fish and Wildlife Service published a study Whitesell believed backed this interpretation of waterfowl population dynamics, he became even more forceful in his opinion, suggesting time and again that season lengths and bag limits should not be restricted, even when duck populations are low. The only result of doing so, Whitesell believed, would be lost interest among hunters, which would mean less revenue for federal and state habitat programs—and for Ducks Unlimited.

"Unfortunately, that study was widely misinterpreted," said Bruce Batt of the Delta Waterfowl Research Centre in Delta, Manitoba. "What it said was that in some instances, when populations of ducks are relatively high, the effect of the gun is probably compensatory, meaning that what birds fall to the gun probably only compensate for birds that would have died naturally.

"But the study was very, very complex, and could not be easily or simply explained in laymen's terms. What the study actually said was that the effect of the gun is probably compensatory at some point, when populations are high, but additive when populations are lower, meaning that bag-limit and season-length restrictions are probably warranted under those conditions."

Under Whitesell, Ducks Unlimited staff and volunteers also repeated frequently the notion that Ducks Unlimited could not take positions on projects such as Garrison in North Dakota because their bylaws prevented them from becoming politically active.

In fact, while the organization's articles of incorporation describe the group as non-political, Ducks Unlimited bylaws include no mention of politics.

"The reason DU has never positioned itself on those resource issues is because they have felt it would hurt them financially," said a source who works closely with the group and who asked not to be named. "Don't get me wrong, they don't come out and say as much, but they know that to be the case.

"Also, their heritage in the United States is that they exist for the sole purpose of raising money. That's changed somewhat now, but for most of their 50 years, that's what they've done. So they haven't really had the people in place who have been accustomed to being politically active.

"But raising money, they do it well. They should, because they're obsessed with it. Obsessed to the point where in some instances they've hurt ducks by traditionally ignoring resource issues other than Canadian nesting habitat? In some instances, yes, that's been the case."

In November 1985, in the midst of falling duck populations, Whitesell wrote an editorial in the Ducks Unlimited magazine entitled "Voodoo Bionomics," in which he challenged the validity of the annual Fish and Wildlife Service duck census, and disagreed with the service's intent to severely restrict season lengths and bag limits in order to reduce the duck harvest in the United States by 25 percent.

But whether Ducks Unlimited leaders and members sided with Whitesell or with the Fish and Wildlife Service, everyone agreed about one thing: There were very few ducks in the sky.

It's a warm spring day in suburban Chicago as Matt Connolly gathers his executive staff in a conference room.

"We are at this time in a strategic planning process that we hope will provide a new direction for the company," Connolly says. "We are looking at a better organizational configuration for both volunteers and staff."

In this, Connolly is in part referring to the size of the executive committee, which, at 61 members—about 45 of whom regularly attend the panel's three meetings each year—is unwieldy.

"We know that," Connolly concedes. "We're looking into it."

But under Ducks Unlimited's current corporate structure, change will come slowly. Most national officers rise through the ranks, beginning at the local level, then rising to zone chairman and so on, until the rank of "trustee" is achieved, which is a position on the group's 260-member board.

In almost all instances, the board relegates the operation of the organization to the executive committee, none of whom, according to Ducks Unlimited policy, can be reimbursed for expenses associated with their position, not even for air travel.

"When I was the top guy in the Atlantic Flyway for Ducks Unlimited," Harry Knight said, "I spent about $15,000 a year out of my own pocket flying around, attending meetings and so forth. Some of our presidents have spent as much as $100,000 or more in a year, again out of their own pockets."

Such restrictions means the top positions in the organization are almost by definition open only to the wealthy.

"To some degree, that's probably true," Knight said.

Connolly believes this will change and believes as well that other changes will come to Ducks Unlimited in the near future, among them:

✓ The organization's contribution to the Wildlife Conservation Fund of America will be "cut back" and perhaps be eliminated.

✓ Ducks Unlimited will in the future advocate positions on resource issues of the kind it has ignored in the past.

"The work the Corps of Engineers is doing on the Yazoo River basin down south will have an adverse impact on ducks, and we likely will oppose that," Connolly said.

Ducks Unlimited Communications Director Charlotte Rush adds that advocacy positions must be chosen carefully. "It's one thing to say we're going to become active on the Yazoo project, it's another to say that we're going to become involved in every little wetlands issue that may come up. What would be troublesome to our membership would be if our attention became diverted from our conservation programs. It's a gut-wrenching and difficult process to come up with positions, and we don't want to diminish our overall effectiveness."

✓ The possibility exists that Ducks Unlimited may soon have a "presence" in Washington, D.C. "Not to lobby so much, perhaps, but to educate, and to work with government officials and agencies whose actions affect ducks," said Connolly.

178

✓ The word is going out to Ducks Unlimited members to expect cutbacks in season lengths and bag limits this fall. "We're willing to make the sacrifice this fall," said Connolly. "But we need other people to make sacrifices, too, and help contribute to the North American Waterfowl Management Program, which is a great blueprint, but which needs a lot of private and governmental help if we're going to return ducks to the level of 100 million birds."

✓ Ducks Unlimited will begin to address more forcefully the issue of hunter behavior. "We've scheduled a symposium for next year in Washington, D.C., and the issue of harvest, illegal as well as legal, will be on the agenda. Also, we've had a slide show developed by a game warden that our field staff will be using at various events. And as I've said before, our fall magazine will have an editorial and article dealing with the issue of hunter ethics."

As Connolly speaks, in a pond just outside, a pair of Canada geese preen themselves. Farther beyond, a hen mallard fends off a trio of aggressive greenheads.

"You've got to realize, there are a lot of new people in this firm right now," Connolly says. "At the same time, there are a lot of seasoned people here who haven't had the opportunity to participate in some of the programs of the company.

"This strategic planning program we are in has given us a great opportunity to suggest some directions for Ducks Unlimited that just had been thought about privately before."

Drought latest threat to waterfowl

SUNDAY, JULY 17, 1988

In prairie Canada—Much of North America's rapidly declining duck population won't breed this year due to a devastating drought that has displaced millions of birds from parched U.S. and Canadian prairies, according to federal waterfowl officials.

The world's best waterfowl biologists and managers, none of whom have ever seen ducks in such straits, are uncertain how to respond. Some who have trekked across Canada's prairies this summer and have seen firsthand the drought's devastation say privately ducks may well be on their way out, the latest species to fall victim to man's ceaseless attack on North American wetlands and farmlands, and his inability or unwillingness to limit hunting, legal as well as illegal. U.S. Fish and Wildlife Service pilots flying duck breeding-population surveys over southern Manitoba, Saskatchewan, and Alberta report these regions are largely devoid of waterfowl.

Traditionally, about 50 percent of North American ducks nest on the U.S. and Canadian prairies. Concentrations of birds are instead being found, according to the pilots, in Canada's northern parklands and in Alaska, where production is expected to be severely reduced.

Surveyors also report that pintails—a favored duck of waterfowlers in Louisiana, Texas, and California—are in a free-fall, their breeding numbers plummeting from 5.4 million in 1980 to about 2.8 million this spring. Other species—including canvasbacks, blue-winged teal, and mallards—are also threatened, as are scaup, which are at their third lowest level on record.

Later this month, when the breeding success of U.S. and Canadian ducks is estimated by Fish and Wildlife Service biologists in Maryland, waterfowl managers will have the information they need to issue a 1988 fall flight forecast. Some observers believe it will be 55 million or below, the lowest on record.

U.S. Fish and Wildlife Service director Frank Dunkle has already moved to close special early teal-hunting seasons first implemented in southern states in the 1960s. And Dunkle said that he will take whatever other steps are necessary to ensure ducks are protected.

"In setting hunting seasons this year, if I'm going to err, I'm going to err on the side of ducks," Dunkle said, noting that some people, including some waterfowl managers, are calling for a complete duck-hunting closure this year.

Rollie Sparrowe, chief of the Fish and Wildlife Service Office of Migratory Bird Management, is Dunkle's top duck manager. Sparrowe understands that while periods of drought are common to prairie regions, he believes the severity and duration of the current dry period pose a particularly severe threat to ducks.

"The problem this year is critical," Sparrowe said. "What is alarming is that, while the breeding population of ducks as a whole isn't significantly lower than last year's, many species' populations were at depressed levels last year, and in years previous. And the drought will significantly reduce production by the birds we do have.

"What's worse, this year's drought is just another year in a long-running dry period on the Canadian prairies, and the cumulative effect of the dry weather on ducks is what especially concerns us.

"There is growing concern, for instance, that the drought will severely affect migration and wintering habitats for ducks. Massive grain crop failures, as an example, will remove vast areas of feed that ducks traditionally use while migrating."

Sparrowe is also concerned that the drought will concentrate ducks in limited areas during migration. This will increase the threat of botulism and other diseases, he said, and make the birds more accessible to hunters.

"There is also recent research to indicate that the condition of ducks when they leave the southern wintering grounds in spring to return north is important to a hen's ability to nest successfully," Sparrowe said.

"This is especially true now, in a time when predators have such an adverse effect on nesting ducks. It's important that if a hen has her nest destroyed by a predator, she has enough strength to attempt a second nesting.

"The possibility that the drought will continue into next year only complicates the equation."

If the drought were to continue, ducks could well be devastated. Already, several of the lowest North American duck breeding population levels on record have occurred in the 1980s.

And three of the five lowest May pond counts—an index of the amount of water available to breeding ducks—have occurred this decade.

In southern Manitoba, west of Portage la Prairie, lies the eastern edge of Canada's prairie pothole region. From there to western Alberta stretches a band of agricultural land that is scarred with millions of depressions.

The geography unique to the pothole region, whose southern border extends to Iowa, was carved out by retreating glaciers, which left in their wake a huge moraine consisting of ice, rock, and soil.

When the moraine melted and settled, it created the region's topography.

In years of average precipitation, Canada's prairie depressions—potholes—are filled with water by early May. As breeding ducks return from their southern wintering grounds, they are attracted to the potholes—most are less than two acres in size—because they warm faster than larger bodies of water and because they are rich in invertebrates and other foods valuable to diets of nesting hens.

This spring, many ducks returning to prairie Canada, and to the prairies of Montana and North and South Dakota, discovered that only the largest of potholes—and those supplied with sufficient amounts of groundwater—contained water.

The remainder were bone dry.

Many ducks continued north until they found water.

Which explains why some Fish and Wildlife Service pilots flying survey routes over prairie Canada this spring had difficulty staying awake. There simply were no ducks or water-filled potholes to count.

"We've known for a long time displaced ducks will not breed, or, if they do, they won't breed very successfully," said Bruce Batt, director of the Delta Waterfowl and Wetlands Research Centre in Delta, Manitoba. "So when the birds were found not on the prairies this spring but in the parklands, we knew production would be poor."

Earlier this summer, Delta's trustees recommended to the Fish and Wildlife Service that hunting seasons this fall be severely restricted, and that hunting of pintails and canvasbacks be banned altogether.

In the 20 years Batt has been at Delta, he's never seen the prairies look so inhospitable to waterfowl. When sustained rains again come to the region, he believes it will once again support millions of breeding ducks.

But he worries that with the continent's duck populations so precariously low, the birds may be unable to rebound in significant numbers when favorable nesting conditions finally return.

He worries also that farmers and other landowners will continue to convert dried potholes to cropland, further reducing the region's duck reproductive capacity.

And what potholes aren't drained in prairie Canada, said Batt, are oftentimes burned.

"Take a picture of that," Batt said last week as he drove by a wetland set afire by a farmer who was plowing a nearby field. "Why is he doing that at this time of year? There's no reason to do it. There's really no reason to do it at any time. But especially not at this time of year.

"The farmer probably just drove by the pothole on his tractor, saw it there all dried out, and the tradition among farmers of burning potholes just became too much for him to resist. So he set it on fire."

Up the road, not far from the burning slough, lay more examples of habitat loss to agriculture. Potholes and other small sloughs that once held water were now crop-filled depressions, part of the farmscape planted in grain and other crops.

Also complicating the situation for ducks on the prairies is the loss of grasslands that once proliferated around potholes, providing valuable protection from predators for nesting waterfowl.

"Because of the loss of upland cover around potholes, predators are very efficient on the prairies," said Mike Anderson, who oversees Delta's research projects at Minnedosa, in southern Manitoba. "Studies have shown that ducks on some parts of the prairies nesting in the uplands have only about a 10 percent nest success rate. Ducks that nest over water do a little better; perhaps 15 to 20 percent of them are successful nesting. The other nests are lost to predators.

"You don't have to travel around up here very much to see why predation is such a problem for ducks. Farmers plow and plant right up to the edge of potholes. Predators know ducks are nesting in the potholes, and they oftentimes just follow their noses to the nest."

Striped skunks, red foxes, raccoons, mink and aerial predators, including crows, magpies, great-horned owls, and hawks, are the most efficient prairie duck-nest robbers and hen killers.

184

Their breeding-duck surveys complete, Dunkle's pilots are once again in the air over North and South Dakota, Montana, Manitoba, Saskatchewan, Alberta, and Alaska, counting birds. This time their mission is to count duck broods (newly hatched young) so federal biologists can estimate as closely as possible the number of ducks that will fly south this fall.

It's this number—the fall flight estimate—that Dunkle will present later this month to state and provincial representatives to the four waterfowl flyway councils: Atlantic, Mississippi, Central, and Pacific.

The councils will consider the fall-flight information and make recommendations by early August for the upcoming hunting seasons.

The Fish and Wildlife Service will consider the recommendations and will establish a national waterfowl-hunting framework within which individual states can set their seasons.

"The brood-count surveys aren't complete yet," Sparrowe said, "but early indications are in from the prairies that show production is way off. If these trends continue, as we suspect they will, significant changes in hunting seasons are likely."

Dunkle agrees.

"We already know there aren't many breeding ducks on the prairies," he said. "If the surveys also show that these ducks had poor nesting success, as we expect they did, then we're going to have to look at a whole series of hunting regulations.

"These include special hunting zones, special seasons, early seasons, late season, the point system, opening hours, season length, daily bag limits, and possession limits.

"All of these things are designed to harvest waterfowl. We'll start to look at the most liberal among them at first and take some action. We're going to have to think first of the ducks, and then see what kind of opportunity we can allow for hunting."

Dunkle and Sparrowe acknowledge the dearth of ducks this fall will be felt disproportionately in different areas of the nation. Louisiana, for instance, which winters in excess of 50 percent of Mississippi and

185

Central flyway ducks, still will be home to millions of waterfowl this fall. The same is true for Mexico, where, as in Louisiana, enforcement of waterfowl regulations has traditionally been lax.

"No one knows how much of an effect hunting has on waterfowl populations," said Batt of the Delta research center. "So no one knows what beneficial effect you can have by restricting hunting. And we don't know how big the take is by illegal hunters because nobody has studied it. So we don't know what, if any, effect that's having on ducks.

"In any case, you have to keep in mind that managing and researching waterfowl, particularly ducks, is very complex and very difficult.

"We think that when ducks are low in number, hunting can adversely affect their population. How much, we don't know. All we know is that we have relatively few ducks right now, and that they will have poor reproduction this year. So it's wise to do the one thing we can do—restrict hunting—just in case it helps the situation."

Further complicating the issue is the fact that duck hunters provide most of the funds for waterfowl management and habitat acquisition in the United States and Canada. The money comes from license and stamp sales, and from a special federal excise tax on guns and other hunting-related equipment.

Should duck hunters lose interest in their sport, figuring ducks are so scarce the time and expense involved in going afield is no longer worth the effort, the continent's entire duck management and preservation systems could crumble.

If this occurs, said Sparrowe, the decline of ducks likely will be precipitous, as hundreds of thousands of acres of U.S. and Canadian wetlands currently preserved to benefit ducks are converted to other uses.

"Hunters should support whatever actions the federal government and the flyway councils end up having to take this fall to protect the resource," Sparrowe said. "It's likely this means giving up some hunting opportunity for the short term with a view toward protecting the resource in the long term.

"Admittedly, there's not much good news for ducks right now. We who manage the birds have the task of keeping everyone's energies and interests up at a time when duck hunting opportunity has to be cut back to protect the future of the birds.

"I know this: If people give up on the sport under a couple of years of restrictive hunting, I can guarantee ducks will go away. Our long-term plan to help ducks recover—the North American Waterfowl Management Plan—will be successful only if people who love ducks are willing to go the extra mile.

"We're just not in a position any more to guarantee continued hunting at recent levels."

187

Donations will put helicopter in Louisiana skies

NOVEMBER 1, 1988

The Izaak Walton League, a conservation organization, has ordered a $600,000 helicopter to help federal wildlife agents protect America's declining duck population from poachers in Louisiana and throughout the Gulf Coast.

The Bell Jet Ranger helicopter was ordered Friday after details of its purchase were agreed to in Washington, D.C., by the league's executive director, Jack Lorenz, and Fish and Wildlife Service director Frank Dunkle. The five-passenger helicopter will be delivered in September 1989.

"We're just delighted the project is nearing a successful conclusion and that ducks will finally get the protective escort they need," Lorenz said. "This says a lot about duck hunters and about the fact that if they want ducks in the future, they're going to have to take care of them."

David Hartwell of Long Lake, Minnesota, also attended Friday's meeting. He represented more than 3,000 people, mostly hunters, who have contributed to the Helicopter Project, a fund-raising campaign begun in March by the *Pioneer Press* and the Izaak Walton League.

The Helicopter Project was launched after the *Pioneer Press* published articles detailing violations of federal waterfowl laws in Louisiana, which winters about one-fourth of North America's ducks.

In the articles, wildlife agents estimated the number of ducks killed

188

illegally by hunters in Louisiana exceeds the number killed legally by as many as four to one. Agents said the illegal kill cannot be controlled in the vast coastal marshes without the use of a pontoon-equipped helicopter.

Outlaw hunters kill excessive numbers of ducks—for example, three Louisiana hunters were tagged in January for illegally killing 168 ducks—by using corn, milo, or rice to "bait" the birds to within shotgun range. Waterfowl baiting has been prohibited by federal law since 1935.

Wildlife agents flying over Louisiana's coastal marsh, which is 50 miles wide and 250 miles long, often can see bait in the water. But they are unable to land fixed-wing aircraft in the marsh to arrest violators.

The first Fish and Wildlife Service helicopter used to protect ducks was leased and assigned to Louisiana in 1963. Agents made 14 landings the first day and arrested 14 parties of hunters. Violations included baiting, use of live decoys, and killing excessive numbers of ducks.

In 1965, the service purchased a helicopter to patrol the Chesapeake Bay area, as well as Louisiana. Three years later, the service purchased a Bell helicopter on floats and assigned it to Louisiana. Dave Hall of Slidell, Louisiana, was among Fish and Wildlife Service special agents assigned to that helicopter.

"It reduced the gross overbagging and baiting tremendously," Hall said. "There are so many helicopters flying over the Louisiana marshes, many belonging to the oil and gas companies, that hunters just couldn't know which one was ours. Consequently, they stopped baiting. When they knew we would land and apprehend, it was all over."

But in 1971, the Bell helicopter was totaled in an accident. Baiting again flourished, and excessive numbers of ducks were killed illegally. It was not until 1977, with the help of Louisiana Senator J. Bennett Johnston, that the federal government appropriated $100,000 to lease a helicopter.

The most famous bust by helicopter in Louisiana may have occurred in 1977, when agents shut down the Schenley Duck Club. Ace

189

Cullum of Monroe, Louisiana, was head guide at Schenley.

"We had 12 blinds, all heavily baited, and we averaged between 50 and 60 mallards per blind per morning," Cullum said. "The federal agents couldn't get to us because we used guards equipped with walkie-talkies who informed us if they saw anything suspicious. In addition, we had people in state government who would tip us off if state wildlife agents were planning to inspect the camp."

Using the leased helicopter, federal agents surprised the Schenley hunters, landing early one morning and arresting hunters who were shooting over bait and had too many birds.

The federal money for the leased helicopter lasted only two seasons, however, and baiting and overkilling flourished thereafter.

At the same time, beginning in 1980, drought hit the Canadian prairies, where more than half of North American ducks are produced each summer. The drought has combined with habitat loss and relatively stable gunning pressure to severely undercut duck populations.

That is why organizers of the Helicopter Project felt the need to raise funds for a new helicopter. In addition to the Izaak Walton League, organizations active in the project included the Minnesota Waterfowl Association, the Wisconsin Waterfowl Association, the Michigan Duck Hunters Association, and the North American Wildlife Foundation.

"A helicopter in Louisiana will help reduce the illegal kill of ducks, that's for sure," said Greg Berg, executive director of the Minnesota Waterfowl Association. "But just as important, and perhaps more important, is the message being sent. And that is this: The old days are gone. Times have changed. Duck hunters have to begin to appreciate the hunting experience in many ways, not just by the number of ducks killed."

Still, wildlife officials found the Helicopter Project to be a difficult undertaking. Some hunters refused to believe illegal hunting contributes to the duck decline. And opposition, at least implicitly, by Ducks Unlimited also slowed contributions.

The biggest contributors have been the Philip Morris Co., which last week pledged $25,000, and the Carl Weyerhauser Charitable Trust, which confirmed a $25,000 donation Friday. The Andersen, Knight, and Bell foundations each contributed $10,000. The largest contribution from an individual—$10,000—was made by real estate developer Orrin Thompson and his son, Gary.

In the agreement signed Friday, the Izaak Walton League, acting as trustee for contributors, pledged $250,000 toward the helicopter purchase. That represents the amount donated or pledged to the project as of Friday. The remaining $341,000, less additional funds contributed before December 15, will be contributed by the Fish and Wildlife Service.

"Never again will there be articles published like those [in the *Pioneer Press*] about Louisiana," Governor Buddy Roemer told a gathering of Louisiana outdoor writers earlier this year. "We fully intend to begin protecting ducks."

Minnesota senators Dave Durenberger and Rudy Boschwitz helped to forge the agreement between the federal agency and the Izaak Walton League. Johnston, the senator from Louisiana, and Minnesota Attorney General Hubert Humphrey III played key roles in writing an amendment to an appropriation bill urging the wildlife service to contribute to the project.

Project sponsors also credited federal agents Hall and Bill Mellor, Louisiana state wildlife agent Roy Chauvin, and Fish and Wildlife Service director Frank Dunkle for their work on the Helicopter Project.

EMPTY SKIES: AMERICA'S DUCKS IN CRISIS
How the helicopter deal was struck

SUNDAY, NOVEMBER 13, 1988

Regular readers of this column will recall articles published in the *Pioneer Press* about duck poaching in Louisiana, as well as articles quoting federal and state agents who work along the Gulf Coast and say they could control the illegal "baiting" of ducks, and therefore their considerable overharvest, if the agents had a helicopter.

After the initial Louisiana stories were published, I floated the idea in a column that, since the Fish and Wildlife Service and its funding agent—Congress—hadn't seen fit in recent years to purchase a helicopter, perhaps the public should.

When hundreds of readers wrote to me in agreement, the project was launched. The month was March. The first week, about $9,000 was contributed.

Thinking (naively, as it turned out) the project could be completed in a relatively short time, maybe two or three months, and thinking as well that a major contributor of $25,000 or more at the outset would help spur contributions of similar size, I organized a small lunch of key conservationists to discuss the issue and arrive at a plan.

About $12,000 was raised at the lunch, the money to be used, it was agreed, to hire a person to coordinate fund-raising for the Helicopter Project.

As it happened, the decision was one of the best made in the campaign, because the person hired, Angie Wozniak Smith of St. Paul, played a critical role in the undertaking. Angie will be with the project until its conclusion.

Also critical at that juncture was the contribution by BCE Development of St. Paul of an office, phone, and secretarial help for Angie. BCE also made a corporate contribution of $5,000 to the Helicopter Project and sponsored a month-long fund-raiser at Saint Paul Center in downtown St. Paul.

In the months since, countless lunches, dinners, and meetings have been held to make people aware of the Helicopter Project, to answer their questions, and to ask for donations. Always a film made by Fish and Wildlife Service special agent Dave Hall of Slidell, Louisiana, was shown; a film bearing in color and almost live the true confessions of Southern duck poachers now reformed.

Concurrent with this effort, the Minnesota congressional delegation was at work in Washington. Their goal was twofold: to include in federal legislation a clause making it legal for the public to give the Fish and Wildlife Service a helicopter (which at the time wasn't legal) and, if possible, to procure federal funding for the helicopter.

In the first matter, the congressional delegation was successful. In the second, it wasn't.

In early August, at a meeting in Senator Dave Durenberger's Washington office that included, at Durenberger's invitation, Fish and Wildlife Service Director Frank Dunkle and me, a plan was developed to seek $400,000 for the helicopter from a House–Senate Interior appropriations committee when it met later that week.

In the meeting, Dunkle insisted he be allowed to reserve $200,000 of the $400,000 for operation and maintenance of the helicopter in its first year of use.

The conference committee was chaired by the powerful and influential Senator J. Bennett Johnston of Louisiana, a friend of Minnesota

Attorney General Hubert H. "Skip" Humphrey III, who about this time offered a plan of his own to seek help from the conference committee for the helicopter.

To implement his plan, Humphrey called on Johnston (like Humphrey, a Democrat) for help.

The fact that Johnston was a friend of Skip Humphrey's late father, Vice-President Hubert H. Humphrey, and that Johnston played a key role in the appropriation in the late 1970s to the Fish and Wildlife Service of $100,000 to lease a helicopter for duck protection, provided Humphrey with an inside track.

Johnston proved friendly to Humphrey's plan, and submitted for approval to the conference committee language developed by Humphrey urging the Fish and Wildlife Service to contribute $400,000 to the Helicopter Project.

The committee approved Johnston's request.

On paper, this meant contributors to the Helicopter Fund would need only to raise $400,000 to buy a $600,000 helicopter, inasmuch as the remainder would be paid by the Fish and Wildlife Service.

But snags arose almost immediately.

One was that the conference committee didn't appropriate an additional $400,000 to the service for the helicopter. Rather, it merely said the service should take the money from its enforcement budget discretionary fund.

What the conference committee didn't know, according to Dunkle, the Fish and Wildlife Service director, was that Dunkle already had plans for his discretionary enforcement budget, and in fact already had committed it to hire and train an extra eight agents so that, as his agent corps was reduced in fiscal 1989 by retirement, attrition, etc., he could have ready replacements.

Because these additional agents had already been hired, Dunkle, in effect, had no discretionary money in his enforcement budget.

"To take [the service's] part of the helicopter money out of that

194

budget, I'd have to lay off those agents," Dunkle said. "I won't do that."

Confusing matters still further, the helicopter business, worldwide, was becoming maddening, as order after order came in to Bell Helicopter Textron in Ft. Worth, Texas—from Japan, from Mexico, from every spot, really, on the globe.

Thus, lead time for building a helicopter increased almost weekly, stretching from 90 days last March to 120, to 150, and beyond.

Jon Wright, a Bell vice-president who has been a Helicopter Project advisor from the outset, told me in early September: "If you don't order that helicopter pretty soon, you won't get one before 1990. In fact, even if you order today [September 8] you won't get it until April 1989."

This was both bad news and good. Bad because if a helicopter couldn't be delivered in the government's fiscal 1989 (October 1, 1988, to September 30, 1989), all deals with the $400,000 appropriation likely would have to be renegotiated.

But the news could be interpreted as good, too, because it meant the Fish and Wildlife Service would not need $200,000 for operation and maintenance of a helicopter if it had the ship for only half of its fiscal year (the period April to September 1989 equaling half the government's fiscal year). In fact, under those circumstances, logic would dictate only $100,000 would be needed for a half-year's operation and maintenance.

"I'll agree to the $300,000–$100,000 split," Dunkle told me in late September, "with $300,000 going to the Helicopter Fund and $100,000 kept for operation and maintenance, if the president signs the [Interior] appropriations bill and *if* I don't have to lay off any agents."

On September 30, President Reagan signed the appropriations bill. But it wasn't until almost a month later that Dunkle, working with Minnesota senators Durenberger and Rudy Boschwitz, as well as Louisiana Senator Johnston and Minnesota Attorney General Humphrey, developed a way to appropriate the $400,000.

The money would come, Dunkle said, from the Fish and Wildlife

Service's administration budget.

Finally, on Monday, October 31, Dunkle told me by telephone from Washington he was prepared to move forward with the $300,000–$100,000 plan previously discussed.

A quick check with Bell Helicopter, however, found orders for choppers still coming in at a rapid pace. Over the weekend of October 29 to 30, for example, Mexico placed an order for five ships.

"The best I can do now," Wright of Bell said Monday, October 31, "is get you a ship in September 1989. But if I don't get the order this week, you won't get one until 1990. And we'll have a price increase by then for sure."

The Helicopter Fund on that Monday had in it cash and pledges totaling about $250,000. Included was a pledge of $25,000 by the Phillip Morris Co., the biggest of the campaign. (Another $25,000 pledge would follow from the Carl Weyerhauser Charitable Trust.)

To bring the Helicopter Project closer to conclusion, a plan was developed by its supporters, including Angie and David Hartwell, Twin Cities conservationists who have been active in the project since its launch last spring.

The idea was that St. Paul attorney David O'Connor, a project volunteer, would develop a proposal to be signed by the Izaak Walton League and the Fish and Wildlife Service calling for the league to contribute a minimum of $250,000 to the helicopter, while the service would contribute $341,000.

The service's share represented $41,000 more than Dunkle had earlier committed. But because the service couldn't get the helicopter until the end of its fiscal year—September 1989—it would need little, if any, money that year for operation and maintenance of the ship.

Also included in the proposal were clauses detailing that the ship was to be owned exclusively by the service and was to be used exclusively, or almost exclusively, for waterfowl protection. Moreover, a clause specifically stated that, when, for whatever reason, the ship is in need of replacement, the service will act quickly to replace it.

On Tuesday, November 1, the proposal was sent by express mail to Dunkle in Washington. He and his staff reviewed it, and in a conversation Thursday, November 3, Dunkle told me the deal was OK. A meeting was set for the next day to finalize the agreement.

Ten minutes after the conversation with Dunkle on Thursday, $25,000 was wired to Bell helicopter Textron in Ft. Worth from the Helicopter Fund at Commercial State Bank in St. Paul. The money represented a down payment on a Bell Jet Ranger helicopter to be delivered in September 1989.

The next day, Friday, November 4, Izaak Walton League director Jack Lorenz, together with Hartwell, met with Dunkle and his staff at the Interior Building in Washington.

The agreement was signed, the deal done.

Slaughter of waterfowl rampant in Texas

SUNDAY, DECEMBER 18, 1988

Houston—U.S. Fish and Wildlife Service special agents Saturday concluded the largest undercover investigation of duck hunters and duck-hunting clubs in the nation's history, documenting more than 1,300 violations of waterfowl hunting regulations along the Texas Gulf Coast over a three-year period.

Agents say violations occurred on 92 percent of 228 undercover hunts conducted.

Even some service veterans said they were stunned by the severity and flagrancy of what they saw.

"The violations are so rampant it's sickening," said an agent who worked undercover during the three years. "At certain times, we brought in agents from the East Coast to work undercover, and they couldn't believe it. It's gotten totally out of hand down here, totally out of control.

"Near Corpus Christi, they're knocking the —— out of the continent's largest remaining concentration of redheads. The wanton waste is unbelievable. They don't even retrieve shovelers down here; they just call them trash ducks.

"On more than one occasion we would see hunters come in from hunting with more than 100 birds in excess of their legal limit. They didn't even attempt to hide the birds. They weren't afraid of anything."

On one hunt, agents posing as hunters filmed the slaughter by 13 hunters of 204 snow geese drawn to a small pond agents suspected was baited with grain.

The geese were shot on the water by the hunters, who were instructed by guides to aim their shotguns through holes in the blinds in order to maximize their concealment, and their potential kill.

On a similar hunt at the same club, 19 hunters killed 171 snow geese. On yet a third hunt, 130 geese were killed by 18 hunters.

When an undercover agent asked a guide at the club how it was so many geese could be attracted to such a small pond that held only a single decoy, he was told by the guide, who did not concede the pond was baited: "We sit right at the apex of the Central Flyway. That's why we get so many birds in this pond."

Approximately 200 business operators and hunters, including a handful of elected public officials and scores of professional hunting guides, will face criminal charges, including 95 felonies, stemming from a raid of Gulf Coast duck clubs Tuesday.

More than half the service's approximately 200 agents, many of them wearing bulletproof vests, participated in the meticulously planned takedown, which occurred without incident.

Charges alleged by the Fish and Wildlife Service against hunters and guides include shooting in excess of legal limits of ducks and geese, selling migratory birds, using electronic bird calls, rallying waterfowl for the purpose of shooting, using lead instead of steel shot, failing to retrieve downed birds, failure to tag downed waterfowl, falsifying tags on downed waterfowl, shooting after legal hours, shooting in closed season, and killing protected species such as raptors, herons, ibises, blue jays, terns, killdeer, larks, plovers, and others.

Three airboats and three vehicles were seized Tuesday. Twenty-three arrest warrants were issued and five search warrants were executed.

199

Texas, with Louisiana and California, is a key state for wintering waterfowl. Pintails, redheads, teal, and snow geese are among the most abundant species in the state from September through March.

Penalties for misdemeanor violations of the Migratory Bird Treaty Act and the Lacey Act alleged by Fish and Wildlife Service agents against the guides, hunters, and businesses include six months to one year in prison and fines of $5,000 to $100,000 for individuals and $10,000 to $200,000 for organizations.

Maximum penalties of alleged Lacey Act felonies are two to five years in prison and fines of $250,000 for individuals and $500,000 for organizations. The Lacey Act prohibits transportation of wildlife taken in violation of federal law. Felony provisions of the Lacey Act are provided if the purchase or sale of wildlife has occurred and its value is in excess of $350.

The investigation centered on the southern Texas Gulf Coast. Most of the land is privately owned and controlled by commercial duck clubs that offer day hunts for fees ranging from $65 to $500.

Of 41 clubs investigated, 40 were found in violation, according to Fish and Wildlife Service agents.

"We went undercover because it was the only way we could get information about the severity of the offenses," said John Gavitt, special agent in charge of the service's Washington-based branch of special operations, which conducted the investigation.

"We had information about what was going on down here, but working overtly we couldn't get into these areas," said Doug Morris, a Fish and Wildlife Service special agent stationed in Houston. "For example, one camp in the area is protected by a levee that can only be crossed with the help of a crane that lifts guides' airboats over the levee and puts them down on the other side. Without working covertly, there's no way we could get into a camp like that."

In a press release issued from Washington, Fish and Wildlife Service director Frank Dunkle decried the alleged actions by Texas hunters and guides.

"Duck numbers already are near record lows because of the drought

200

and continued destruction of their natural habitat. They cannot long withstand additional losses from illegal harvest. The U.S. Fish and Wildlife Service will not tolerate violations of the waterfowl hunting regulations."

North America's duck population has dropped 60 percent in the last four decades due to pesticides, overgunning, habitat loss, and drought. The most recent estimated fall flight of 66 million ducks was the second lowest on record.

In February, the *Pioneer Press* published a series of articles detailing gross violations of state and federal waterfowl hunting regulations by hunters in Louisiana. Subsequent articles described similar violations by American hunters in Mexico.

In the Louisiana articles, federal agents estimated the number of ducks killed illegally by hunters in Louisiana exceeded those killed legally by four to one.

Some state and federal waterfowl biologists and managers disputed the enormity of the estimated illegal duck kill in Louisiana. But allegations by Fish and Wildlife Service agents working in Texas the last three years, if substantiated, indicate the Gulf Coast illegal waterfowl kill is, as one agent described it, "without limit."

For example:

✓ During the Texas investigation, each time a duck-hunting guide accompanied an agent into the field, the incident was documented as an "occurrence."

"Violations by guides were documented by agents in 320 such occurrences, or 88 percent of the time the guides were with agents," Gavitt said.

✓ "Reordering" of bags under the now-suspended "point" system occurred 88 percent of the time that it allowed hunters to kill more birds.

Reordering occurs when hunters realign the sequence in which they shoot duck species of various point values.

201

✓ The percentage of hunters taking more than their limits during undercover hunts was 41 percent.

✓ The percentage of evening hunts occurring after guides knew limits were already taken by hunters in the morning was 77 percent.

"I'll say this, people down here know how to kill birds," one undercover agent said. "They use bait, electronic callers, whatever it takes."

One guide told undercover agents: "We'll have a little assistance next time you're here. We'll use an electronic caller. It makes a difference between night and day. The wardens and duck hunters will be gone. I made a living for two years like that."

Another guide told an agent: "I'm ashamed to tell you, but once I killed 1,067 doves in one day with this gun." The guide indicated five cases of shells were used to kill the doves. He also said he and eight hunters averaged 100 geese per day for eight consecutive days.

Yet another guide told an agent: "We have some super duck hunting. It's unbelievable. [Your hunters] should limit out every day. They can shoot the guide's [limit]. Last Saturday, I had two guys in the blind. They shot 16 ducks in 15 minutes. All wigeons and pintails. My party last weekend went home with 100 pounds of fillets and 90 ducks."

Gavitt said his agents did not illegally "entrap" any of the hunters or guides during the investigation.

"Entrapment occurs when a person is not predisposed toward committing a crime, but is additionally enticed and encouraged to commit a crime," Gavitt said. "At no time did our agents ask people to commit crimes unless they were totally predisposed to do so."

Asked how duck hunting along the Texas coast could get so out of hand, David Palmer, field operations supervisor of the Texas Department of Parks and Wildlife, said: "Most violations the federal agents found would not be apparent to uniformed officers. Without an undercover unit, it would be difficult to find out what's actually going on at these camps. We have only about 120 game wardens for the entire state of Texas, with another 30 in school.

"It's not that we've slacked off our protection of ducks. We just don't have enough people to do everything. Still, the real answer to the problem is not catching everyone. What we have to do is to change attitudes among hunters. We have to do it through our [*Parks and Wildlife*] magazine, through TV and radio public service commercials, through presentations to schools and service groups."

Gavitt said hunters were checked by state enforcement officers on only five of the 228 undercover hunts.

One guide told an agent, "The odds of getting caught are 100 to 1."

Another guide, watching an approaching boat, told an agent, "If it was a game warden coming, we would pull out and run over him. . . . The next time you're down here, we'll just kill a couple of game wardens."

The accused hunters, guides, and club owners will be tried in federal courts in Texas.

Traditionally, judges vary widely in sentences given to convicted game-law violators, a fact especially true among judges who do not weigh violations against wildlife for what they are, according to Fish and Wildlife Service special agent David Hall of Slidell, Louisiana.

"These are crimes against not just wildlife, but against society," Hall said. "I know this: If anyone in Louisiana were convicted of crimes of the magnitude found in Texas, they'd be sitting in prison a long, long time."

Hall was referring to instances like one told by a Texas guide to an undercover agent in which the guide said he and a friend killed 138 pintails in one day.

The guide indicated his friend would look at the birds flying and say, "I just can't quit shooting."

Louisiana cracking down on illegal duck hunting

SUNDAY, DECEMBER 25, 1988

Baton Rouge, LA—In an unprecedented about-face, the Louisiana Department of Wildlife and Fisheries has in recent months significantly increased its protection of wintering ducks in Louisiana, and is attempting to educate state duck hunters about the threat illegal hunters pose to North America's dwindling duck populations.

The U.S. Fish and Wildlife Service also has intensified waterfowl-law enforcement in Louisiana, adding two agents to its previous resident cadre of seven, and moving a pilot-agent and his small vintage helicopter from Florida to Louisiana.

These actions notwithstanding, severe cash shortages facing the state of Louisiana and especially the state's Department of Wildlife and Fisheries because of depressed oil and gas markets will result on January 2 in the department losing more than 175 positions, 38 in its enforcement division alone.

The cutbacks could offset the recent heightened enforcement efforts in Louisiana, where about a quarter of North America's ducks spend the winter.

Gross violations of state and federal waterfowl hunting laws were detailed in a series of articles published by the *Pioneer Press* in February.

New Louisiana Governor Buddy Roemer was "embarrassed" by the stories and by the fact that previous administrations made little or no effort to protect waterfowl in Louisiana, Roemer aide Manny Fernandez said in a recent interview.

The Louisiana Department of Wildlife and Fisheries, headed by 38-year-old Virginia Van Sickle, has been specifically mandated by Roemer to apprehend hunters who exceed their legal limits of ducks or engage in illegal duck-hunting activities such as baiting.

Roemer appointed Van Sickle secretary of the Wildlife and Fisheries Department in March.

Along with other Gulf Coast states, including Texas, Louisiana has long been considered a haven for outlaw waterfowl hunters. Two of the continent's four flyways, the Central and the Mississippi, converge in Louisiana.

Fernandez said Governor Roemer also has ordered the Louisiana State Police to assign a helicopter to Department of Wildlife and Fisheries enforcement officers for use in apprehending waterfowl-law violators during the 1988–89 Louisiana duck season, which is now open. The helicopter has been equipped with a borrowed set of floats and is capable of landing on Louisiana's vast coastal marsh.

In the *Pioneer Press* stories, federal agents said they could greatly reduce big illegal kills of ducks if they had a helicopter to patrol Louisiana's coastal marshes, which represent about 40 percent of all such marshes in the United States. Readers of the newspaper subsequently contributed about $300,000 to a special fund and joined with the Fish and Wildlife Service to purchase a $600,000 helicopter, which will be delivered to the service in September.

"When I came to this department, I told the governor my number-one priority was game-law enforcement," Van Sickle said in an interview in her Baton Rouge office. "That's why we got the helicopter, and that's why we've been making other positive steps in the enforcement area. I think we're making significant progress."

As part of the Department of Wildlife and Fisheries' recent emphasis on waterfowl law enforcement, Van Sickle has

✓ Attempted to take politics out of the department's hiring process by organizing merit panels to determine job candidate eligibility.

In the past, particularly in the enforcement division, jobs were often given to friends of state legislators, a practice that allowed some Louisiana politicians to kill ducks with virtual impunity. "The politicization of the Department of Wildlife and Fisheries was very demoralizing to the staff," Van Sickle said. "Many wildlife agents did their jobs catching violators, but when nothing came of their work—when charges were later dropped or when, for whatever reason, they never came to court—the officers could see that the system wouldn't support their efforts."

✓ Recruited a Louisiana assistant attorney general to oversee the Department of Wildlife and Fisheries enforcement division.

✓ Implemented a new ticket-tracking system designed to ensure tickets given wildlife law violators do not conveniently "get lost" en route to prosecution. "An agent or anyone else that tampers with tickets today will lose his job and be prosecuted as well," Van Sickle said.

✓ Used roadblocks to check for violators illegally transporting game and fish.

✓ Approved the wearing of camouflage by enforcement agents who before were required to wear uniforms. Van Sickle also has purchased unmarked cars for some officers.

✓ Encouraged Louisiana Department of Wildlife and Fisheries agents to work with special agents of the Fish and Wildlife Service to enforce migratory bird regulations.

In past years, federal agents said they hesitated to work with certain Louisiana agents because the state agents feared for their jobs if a politician or other important Louisiana resident was among the hunters apprehended. Also, some state agents were ordered to "snitch" to their superiors about planned federal waterfowl busts.

✓ Developed television public-service announcements to inform hunters of the depleted status of ducks and to warn hunters not to poach.

206

✓ Organized seminars involving state wildlife agents, federal wildlife agents, federal magistrates, and U.S. attorneys, so "the entire system can work as it should work," Van Sickle said.

✓ Supported a bill passed by the Louisiana Legislature in its last session requiring wildlife-law violators to pay reparations to the state in amounts equaling the value of illegally taken wildlife.

"As much as we didn't like to see the stories about the problems with illegal hunting in Louisiana, in a way they have actually made it easier for us to do what we have had to do to correct the situation," Van Sickle said. "A lot of people have been awakened by the horror stories."

Traditionally, the illegal harvest of ducks has been downplayed by private conservation groups and by state and federal waterfowl managers. But many experts now agree the issue is vital because North America's duck population is near an all-time low, and because breeding populations must be maintained until rains return to drought-plagued northern nesting grounds—helping ducks to rebound at least somewhat—and until lost habitat can be restored.

"[Ducks] cannot long withstand additional losses from illegal harvest," Fish and Wildlife Service Director Frank Dunkle said December 13 when his agents concluded a three-year investigation of Texas hunting clubs. The agents documented violations on 92 percent of 228 undercover hunts conducted in Texas.

Worried that ducks could plummet to population levels from which they could never recover, Fish and Wildlife Service waterfowl managers this year sharply restricted hunting regulations in an effort to reduce the rate of kill by at least 25 percent from the approximately 9 million ducks hunters killed in 1987–88.

The Fish and Wildlife Service also intensified its enforcement of waterfowl laws throughout the nation. For example, one task force of approximately 70 state and federal agents was assigned to Minnesota during the opening weeks of the recently concluded duck season. It was the first such enforcement group assembled in any state.

Similar task forces have been assigned to central and southern states as their waterfowl hunting seasons have opened. And more than 100 federal agents participated in the bust of 40 Texas waterfowl hunting camps December 13.

University of Wisconsin–La Crosse professor Robert Jackson, a researcher of hunter behavior, believes the violation of waterfowl laws occurs in every state. But Jackson says it is largely a crime of opportunity and more likely to proliferate in states such as Louisiana and Texas, where large numbers of ducks and geese congregate for several months a year.

Indeed, the entire Cajun culture of the Louisiana marshes was in large part shaped by the ready availability of ducks, geese, shrimp, fish, and crabs, as well as muskrat, nutria, and other furbearers.

But the overharvest in Louisiana of waterfowl—by urban hunters as well as Cajuns—combined with a loss of breeding habitat in northern states and provinces, lax management by state and federal wildlife officials, and the relatively recent—but gravely ominous—erosion of Louisiana's coastal marshes, imperil not only marsh wildlife but entire Louisiana cultures and lifestyles.

"It's going, it's going," said Dennis Treitler, a Cajun who lives along Bayou la Loutre in St. Bernard's Parish. A onetime market hunter of ducks and now a reformed poacher, Treitler routinely visits schools preaching conservation. A broad-chested man, Treitler also patrols marshes near his home, making sure no one shoots too many ducks.

"For as long as anyone can remember, people who live in this area have made a living off the land, market-hunting ducks, trapping, shrimping, crabbing," Treitler said. "Now the marsh is eroding fast. Because the oil and gas companies were allowed to cut so many channels in the marsh, and because the Corps of Engineers lied to us about the channels they built, saltwater is rushing into areas that before were only freshwater. Ducks no longer have places to feed and rest. Shrimp and fish are being hurt, too.

"This is our life I'm talking about down here. I'm not trained to do

208

anything else, and neither are other people who live in the marshes. We can't go into town and get jobs. We're shrimpers, crabbers, whatever. No one around here knows anything else. And it's not half as bad now as it's going to be if the marsh is allowed to continue to erode."

Garland Rolling, a New Orleans attorney and long-standing member of the Little Lake Club, one of Louisiana's oldest duck hunting clubs, shares Treitler's concern about the marsh.

On a recent morning, in a Little Lake Club duck blind on 10,000 acres of prime marshland just south of Lafitte, Louisiana, Rolling told a visitor his camp recently received a $165,000 out-of-court settlement from Texaco for damage done to club marshland while the company explored for oil.

"We plowed every cent of it back into the marsh, building levees and trying to keep the saltwater out," Rolling said. "We know if saltwater is allowed to continue into our marsh, we won't have any ducks in a few years. It's as simple as that.

"And when you consider that in Louisiana we're losing two acres of freshwater marsh an hour, you get a feeling for the enormity of the problem—not only on a state level, but on a national level. This is a national resource."

Rolling also echoed Virginia Van Sickle's belief that times are changing for duck hunters in Louisiana.

"More change has occurred among duck hunters and their attitudes in the last six months in Louisiana than in the previous 60 years," Rolling said. "At one time not long ago poaching of ducks was considered socially acceptable. Now it's socially unacceptable.

"We're not proud of it, but the truth is a few years ago four of our members were apprehended by a federal agent. Three of those people are no longer members. And today, if someone came back into camp with more than his limit of ducks, there would be hell to pay.

"We're learning. Everyone's learning. You've got to take care of a resource if you want to keep it.

"Sure, most people in Louisiana didn't like to read the stories about how bad things are for ducks in Louisiana. But it was all true. And we're going to do what we can to change it."

EMPTY SKIES: AMERICA'S DUCKS IN CRISIS
Attitudes are changing in Louisiana

SUNDAY, DECEMBER 2, 1990

Bayou LaFourche, LA—Fifty-three-year-old John Lombas rises early Saturday, November 17, the opening of the 1990 Louisiana waterfowl season. He and his son, Robert, son-in-law John Lerrille Jr., and a companion, Garret Gilliam, plan to take the elder Lombas's mudboat into Louisiana's coastal marsh for a morning duck hunt.

The black sky is clear as Lombas climbs into his boat, the air warm. An afternoon temperature of nearly 70 degrees is predicted, with only slight winds. Weather-wise, it won't be a particularly good duck hunting day.

Still, John Lombas knows ducks will fly over his decoys. To ensure it, he has baited the pond in recent days with 600 pounds of corn.

But Lombas, of Galliano, Louisiana, in Lafourche Parish, doesn't know his pond has for days been watched by U.S. Fish and Wildlife Service special agents.

Earlier in the week, while flying Louisiana's coastal wetlands in a float-equipped Piper Super Cub (the government had seized the plane from poachers in Montana), pilot-agent Bill Mellor of Metairie, Louisiana, saw ducks concentrated in Lombas's pond.

An experienced marshman, Mellor knows how baited ducks behave. And the birds bunched onto Lombas's pond, Mellor knew, were baited ducks.

The night before the opener, in a room at the Ramada Inn in Houma, Louisiana, 13 Fish and Wildlife Service and Louisiana state Department of Wildlife and Fisheries agents had gathered around detailed topographic maps of the marsh where Lombas's pond is located.

Outside the room, on the blacktop moat surrounding the motel, were parked all manner of unmarked enforcement vehicles and watercraft, including a 16-foot Boston Whaler outfitted with a 150-horsepower outboard; two aluminum flatboats (also equipped with high-powered motors); and a 24-foot-long, custom-built airboat powered by a 454-cubic-inch Chevrolet engine.

Surveying the gear, Fish and Wildlife Service special agent Dave Hall of Slidell, Louisiana, said, "Over the years, a lot of outlaw hunters have been caught by agents staying at this motel."

Because it has been illegal since 1935 to hunt baited ducks (ducks coming to corn or other feed lose their natural wariness), Lombas's pond is high on the agents' hit list for opening morning.

Their plan calls for Mellor and Hall to be in the airboat, lying in wait about a mile from Lombas's pond. In the Boston Whaler, Fish and Wildlife Service senior resident agent Jim Bartee will transport Fish and Wildlife Service agent Gene Moore and Louisiana state agent Chuck Comeaux to a location as near the pond as possible. From there, the two agents will paddle to the hunters' blinds in pirogues.

The idea is for Moore and Comeaux to lie secretly in the marsh near the hunters. They will observe the hunters' activities, count ducks downed (noting the time shots are taken), and communicate in whispers by radio to Mellor and Hall, who will be called to help apprehend the hunters.

A third element of the plan involves Fish and Wildlife Service helicopter pilot-agent Ted Curtis, who along with Louisiana state agent Sammy Martin will lift off from the Houma airport at dawn. Curtis and Martin will fly support for the agents working Lombas's pond, as well as two other teams of state and federal agents elsewhere in the marsh.

"Even with good plans, things go wrong," Mellor said as the agents ended their meeting. "A lot of things happen you can't imagine."

The agents ate dinner at a nearby restaurant and returned to their rooms at 10:30 P.M.

They set their alarms for 1:30 A.M.

Also on Friday in southeast Louisiana—on Bayou Gauche—Dennis Badeaux and Tommy Tregle were preparing for opening day.

But they wouldn't be hunting ducks. That privilege had been revoked by a federal magistrate in New Orleans, who earlier in the year found Badeaux and Tregle guilty of shooting more than 50 birds, mostly mallards, over a baited pond.

Badeaux and Tregle had organized the outlaw hunt last January for two Alabama friends. The Alabama men, a lawyer and his father, had hosted Badeaux and Tregle on a deer hunt, and Badeaux and Tregle invited their friends to Bayou Gauche to return the favor.

Badeaux and Tregle did not know at the time of the hunt that federal agents had spotted their baited pond from the air. Nor did they know the same agents twice had sneaked into the pond, once by helicopter, once by airboat, to gather samples of the bait as evidence. The men only knew that when they stopped shooting, 52 dead ducks were spread among their decoys.

It was then that federal agents encircled them. In pirogues. In a helicopter.

Instinctively, Badeaux and Tregle broke for the deep cypress swamp, as many bayou residents traditionally have done when confronted by wildlife agents.

"Had we been alone, we would have given it a try," Badeaux says now. "But we had our friends from Alabama in the blind. We couldn't leave them."

In addition to revoking waterfowl hunting rights for three years, the magistrate fined Badeaux and Tregle each about $1,300, ordered

213

them to perform 300 hours of public service, and committed each to serve 30 days in a halfway house.

On the eve of the 1990 Louisiana duck season, Tregle and Badeaux stood along Bayou Gauche and contemplated events of the past year.

"We did wrong, we admit that," Badeaux said. "It's just that for so long, killing ducks like we did was the accepted practice down here. Nobody thought anything about it. We killed what we wanted to kill. We ate it all. Poule de Eau [French for "chicken of the water," or coots]. We like those as much as anything. We'd kill 200, maybe 300 a day. No big deal."

Said Hall, the Fish and Wildlife Service agent: "Cajuns are the best marshmen in the world. Throughout time, they've been revered for their hunting and trapping skills. The ones that could get away from wildlife agents, they were revered even more. They were heroes."

But after Tregle and Badeaux were busted last year, Tregle's young son was chided at school, indicating that times and attitudes are changing in Louisiana.

Returning from classes, the boy asked his father, "Why did you do that? Why did you kill all those ducks? I'll hunt. But I'm not going to kill over the limit."

Like most Cajuns, Tregle is proud, with strong family ties.

It was unacceptable that he had embarrassed his son.

"I won't do that again," he said.

At 4:30 A.M. on opening day, federal agent Moore and state agent Comeaux settle into their pirogues on the edge of Lombas's pond. With little wind to deter them, mosquitoes buzz about the agents' heads and necks, a hazard of the job.

About two miles away, Mellor and Hall wait in the airboat, the big Chevy engine silent. Bartee, in the Boston Whaler, is nearby.

Mellor and Bartee will ease their boats nearer to the pond after sunup.

Though still dark, the marsh already is alive. Ducks. Egrets. Ibis. Herons. Nutria. Each is well awake, their motions and sounds chaotic—a blue-winged teal darting here, a nutria crying over there.

The groan of hunters' mudboats and other watercraft also can be heard throughout the marsh, as Louisiana's most revered sporting season—duck hunting—begins anew for another year.

One of the mudboats carries John Lombas, his 34-year-old son, 28-year-old son-in-law, and 17-year-old friend.

The four arrive at their pond a little after 5:00 A.M., settling into their blinds apparently without sensing the presence of Moore and Comeaux.

Legal shooting begins about 6:00 A.M.

At 5:43, one of the four hunters fires the first round of the day. Other shots follow, as ducks, addicted to the corn Lombas placed in the pond, circle the blinds in a fashion that brings to mind the term "shooting gallery."

Moore and Comeaux chronicle the action in notebooks, gathering information that later will be used in court. Duck after duck is being killed. Mallards. Spoonbills. Teal. Bluebills. But what strikes Moore and Comeaux as odd, inasmuch as bayou people are usually excellent wingshots, is that the four hunters are having difficulty hitting birds.

The hunters quit shooting about 7:00 A.M., a fact Moore and Comeaux report by radio to Bartee and Mellor.

As Lombas and the others retrieve their ducks, preparing to leave, Mellor fires up the airboat and Bartee cranks the Whaler's big outboard. The two begin closing the distance between themselves and the hunters.

When Moore radios that the four hunters are in their mudboat and are following a watery channel out of the pond, Mellor guns the airboat, its thundering engine propelling the craft in the manner of a low-flying fighter jet.

Open water, levees, dense marsh—Mellor's airboat eats up all of it

215

in big chunks.

Hall, riding shotgun, braces himself for the bumpy ride.

Lombas sees the airboat and throttles additional gas to his mudboat's air-cooled engine. But there's no outrunning Mellor's airboat.

Lombas backs down.

In the helicopter, Agents Curtis and Martin follow the action by radio, landing in a short while on the edge of Lombas's pond.

Mellor, Moore, and the other agents count the hunters' ducks, pulling them from bags in Lombas's boat.

Hall, using a video camera, commits the apprehension to tape.

The tally is 48 ducks and one gallinule, all killed in about an hour and 15 minutes.

The party's legal duck limit would have been 12.

Lombas admits he baited the pond.

"You have to if you want to get ducks these days," he says.

In addition to exceeding their limits, the hunters are cited for hunting over bait, using lead shot, and shooting before legal hours.

Bridling at being filmed by Hall, Lerille says, "How much would it cost me if I make you eat that camera?"

Hall keeps filming.

"More than you'll ever be able to pay," Mellor says.

But the mood soon turns friendly.

"What's going to happen to us?" Robert Lombas asks.

"That's up to the court," an agent says. "But you'll probably lose your hunting rights. And you might do some time in jail."

"Jail?" Robert Lombas says. "For killing ducks?"

Hall says: "It's a serious offense. And it's no longer acceptable. Here, or anywhere."

Minnesota

Wednesday, not far west of Clontarf, a cold rain pelted the plowed fields that border the asphalt of Highway 9. It was late March the way many Minnesotans living on the prairie have come to know late March, a hard-edged wind propelling dead brush out of yet-frozen ditches, dark sky overhead.

The sign that introduces Clontarf to highway visitors coming from Benson or, farther back still, Willmar, claims a resident population of about 200. But that figure doesn't include the thousands of mallards and Canada geese that on Wednesday circled tightly as if caught up by a cyclone, lifting higher and higher before dropping into the plowed remains of last year's cornfield. All of this not two miles east-northeast of Clontarf.

In the center of the field was a large pond, and as a visitor stepped from his truck, collar turned against the wind, binoculars in hand, a pair of tundra swans flew just barely atop the blackened soil and set down gracefully on the water. The presence of the big birds, which, from a distance, appeared pure white, seemed to have a settling effect on the ducks and geese. Soon a pair of mallards, a hen and a drake, set their flaps, cupping the wind and dropping from the sky precipitously. These were followed by another pair and another and another until maybe 500 migrants were atop the water, the birds alternately preening and displaying, resting once more before continuing their spring trip north.

217

If the idea of birds flying north to south in autumn and back again in spring is one you find compelling, you find a reason to be in western Minnesota or the Dakotas or even prairie Canada at the appropriate time. In fall, hunting is the excuse. But in many ways, spring is actually the better time. The birds are more fully and more colorfully plumed, and the flocks are oftentimes more concentrated, bunched up, really, as they follow the receding winter north.

"There have been lots of birds moving through, quite a few mallards, but geese mostly, thousands and thousands of geese," said Brad Svea, a Morris businessman. Svea, with about 425 other Stevens County residents, had attended a conservation dinner the night before in Morris, and it was there that talk centered on birds. Pheasants. Ducks. Geese. Swans. These and others.

"Last fall, I had my yellow Lab down at Lac qui Parle with us, hunting," Svea was saying. "One of my partners winged a honker, and the bird must have sailed a third of a mile. But the dog found the bird."

Svea's story carried no punch line, but it was significant because it indicated what people in this part of Minnesota consider important: pheasant in a farmer's grove; geese moving up the Pomme de Terre; swans flying high overhead, seeking the lesser resistance offered only by thin air. These and other winged creatures provided fodder for conversation in Morris.

"I think we've been hurt a little by the winter out here. I think the pheasants have been hurt a little," said John Scharf, a Department of Natural Resources wildlife manager. "The winter was long and a couple of the storms were pretty bad. But we don't really know how the birds are faring, not yet. It'll be a while before we can tell for sure."

The visitor was thinking about all this as he watched thousands of ducks and geese and swans circle a pond.

Wanting to share the experience, the visitor uncrated three Labradors from the back of his truck. Sensing from the sound of the honking geese, above and in the middle distance, that something neat was about to happen, the dogs pranced with urgency to a spot in front of the truck where the visitor posted them one to his left, two to his right.

From that vista the visitor watched through binoculars as the dogs, eyes fixed to the distant flutter of wings, leaned forward on their haunches, hoping for a freeing command that never came.

It was late March the way many Minnesotans living on the prairie have come to know late March, a hard-edged wind propelling dead brush out of yet-frozen ditches, dark sky overhead.

And plenty of birds in the air.

Photo © by Craig Borck

About the Author

Exploring the outdoors has always been a high priority for Dennis Anderson. He describes his undergraduate education at the University of Minnesota–Morris as "equal parts hunting and reading." Since 1978 he has been writing for the *St. Paul Pioneer Press*. As the paper's outdoors editor he has hunted, fished, and camped his way through Latin America, Alaska, England, and New Zealand.

For his series "Empty Skies: Ducks in Crisis," Anderson was honored as a Pulitzer Prize finalist and winner of the Edward J. Meeman National Journalism Award, given by the Scripps Howard News Foundation for the best environmental reporting in a major U.S. newspaper. Through his newspaper column, he also helped found in 1982 the national conservation group Pheasants Forever.